living in color

living in color

suzy chiazzari

HARPER
DESIGN
international

An Imprint of HarperCollins*Publishers*

contents

LIVING IN COLOR

Copyright © 2004 by Axis Publishing Ltd.

First published throughout the World in English in 2004 by Harper Design International

An imprint of HarperCollins*Publishers*
10 East 53rd Street
New York, NY 10022
www.harpercollins.com

Created and conceived by
Axis Publishing Ltd
8c Accommodation Road
London NW11 8ED
UK
www.axispublishing.co.uk

Creative Director: Siân Keogh
Editorial Director: Anne Yelland
Managing Editor: Conor Kilgallon
Art Director: Clare Reynolds
Designer: Sean Keogh
Production Manager: Toby Reynolds
Production Controller: Jo Ryan

HarperCollins books may be purchased for educational, business, or sales promotional use. For information, please write: Special Markets Department, HarperCollins*Publishers* Inc., 10 East 53rd Street, New York, NY 10022.

First edition

Printed and bound in China

1 2 3 4 5 6 7 / 10 09 08 07 06 05 04

Library of Congress Cataloging-in-Publication Data

Chiazzari, Suzy.
   Living in color / by Suzy Chiazzari.
      p. cm.
   Includes index.
   ISBN 0-06-058925-6 (pbk. with flaps)
   1. Color in interior decoration. 2. Color—Psychological aspects. I. Title.
   NK2115.5.C6C47 2004
   747'.94—dc22
                    2004011770

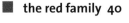

introduction

Sunlight is a powerful energy that nourishes the body and mind. However, it is the individual colors of the rainbow that enrich our lives and make our planet a wonderful place to be. Colors move, sparkle, and excite; sometimes they are joyful and at other times, moody. But they always have a special quality that is essential for life.

Color affects everything we see, think, and do, and exposure to all the colors of the spectrum is essential for physical and mental health. Over 90 percent of information coming into our bodies is through our eyes, but we also absorb light energy through our skin and even breathe in color vibrations from the air around us. By day, sunlight energizes the mind and body so that we can lead active lives. At night, the moon reflects a soft glow that harmonizes our biorhythms and helps us to rest. Living in a colorful environment is an important way in which we harness these life-giving properties to enjoy a happy and healthy existence.

above Different colors in the same room invoke different reactions and create different atmospheres. Light blue is cool and makes a room look larger, reflecting the open, airy expanses of the sky.

above Violet is intense and luxurious, but different effects can be created by using different tones. Saturated tones appear deep and mysterious; lighter ones are gentle and uplifting.

Living in Color takes you on a journey through the world of color, enabling you to learn its language and understand how to use it to express your personality and enhance your moods. Every color has a personality and affects space in a different way, so you will discover how families of color can be used in various situations to create looks and moods. Making friends with color will enable you to develop your own sense of color and discover which colors uplift and inspire you.

Our reactions to different colors are often strong and immediate, and the effects of exposure to certain colors at home and work are powerful and long lasting. It is therefore important that they are chosen carefully. The colors you choose for your home affect the way you live and maximize your home's potential so that you can enjoy it to the full. The right colors can improve the way you use different areas of your home. It can be difficult to imagine color schemes precisely as you have to get a feel for a room. However, through the inclusion of inspiring room-sets, *Living in Color* shows you how to mix and balance the colors like a professional.

Working with color is fun and you should not be afraid to experiment. Color schemes are not permanent: you can refresh any room simply by repainting a wall, while seasonal colors can be added when you feel like a change. Successful color schemes bring together many elements in a harmonious way and allow you to put your stamp on a building without losing its unique essence.

Everyone has a personal relationship with color; there are colors we like and colors we do not like. However, often we live with colors we find unattractive because we lack the confidence to try something new. It is only when you come to understand the true spirit of color that you can create inspiring schemes for your home that not only look good, but make you feel good too.

above Yellow is vibrant and energetic. It is light and bright, energizing the mind while also creating a glow of natural warmth. Its golden hues symbolize wealth, wisdom, and contentment.

the
power of color

Color is energy. It has the power to bring change, joy, and a sense of both physical and mental well-being into the world. Through its universal language we can talk to each other and use it as a means of creative expression. The colors around us also have a profound effect on the way we live and enjoy our homes. But a successful color scheme doesn't just happen by itself; you need to learn how to "color talk" and understand how color harmony works before you can choose and mix color combinations with confidence and create a happy, vibrant home.

The color wheel can help us to understand the theory of color and create color schemes that work. Colors are arranged on the color wheel in the order that they appear in the visible spectrum (as in a rainbow)—

color **talk**

Color talks, but to make sure we like what it is saying, we have to learn its language. The color wheel helps us to translate.

Complementary colors lie opposite each other on the color wheel. Every color has a complement. For the primary colors—red, yellow, and blue—the complementary pairs are red and green, yellow and violet, and blue and orange. Complementary colors balance and excite one another. You can use them to create lively contrasts and dramatic effects. They also hold the balance between hot and cool hues.

from red, the longest wavelength, to violet, the shortest. It shows the relationships between them and how new hues are formed.

The three primary colors are red, yellow, and blue. They make up a triangle on the spokes of the color wheel. These are the three basic hues that cannot be made from any other color and are the building blocks from which all other colors are derived.

Halfway between the three primaries are the secondary hues: orange, green, and violet. These are formed by mixing together two primary colors. Orange is made from red and yellow; green from yellow and blue; and violet from blue and red. Tertiary colors are mixtures of primary and secondary hues, and form another triangle on the color wheel.

SECONDARY COLOR
ORANGE

Orange is a secondary color made up of red and yellow. It can be combined with its complementary color, blue, to create a warm and exciting effect. When combined with pale, neutral colors, it creates a calmer, more soothing effect.

PRIMARY COLOR
YELLOW

Yellow is one of the three primary colors and works well with its neighbor, green. Its complementary color on the opposite side, violet, provides a strong, eye-catching contrast, but not one that many people would find relaxing or soothing.

SECONDARY COLOR
GREEN

Green is a mixture of blue and yellow, so the green color family reveals a combination of character traits. On the one hand, green imbues a room or space with a sense of calm and personal retreat, but the more green tends toward yellow, the more fresh and alive it becomes.

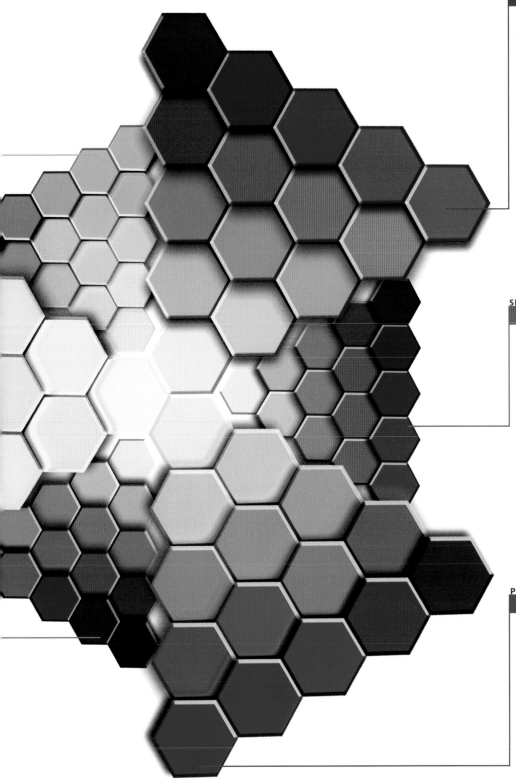

PRIMARY COLOR
RED

The most powerful of the primary colors, red can be used to create a range of moods, from the comforting and cozy, to the dramatic and regal. When paired with its complementary color, green, the resulting clash creates a strobe effect unless you use a variety of tones.

SECONDARY COLOR
VIOLET

Violet, which is made up of red and blue, complements yellow to produce an almost palpable contrast that is warm, rich, and luxurious. However, for many people, this combination can be too overpowering unless diluted with neutrals.

PRIMARY COLOR
BLUE

Blue can work well with its immediate neighbor, violet, but care is needed to select the right hues. Blue and green—a little farther along the color wheel—is a classic color mismatch that is often found in nature and also looks good inside.

hues and **saturation**

Hue is another word for color. Spectrum colors are called pure hues, but when black or white is added they are just known as hues.

Saturation refers to the purity of a hue. When fully saturated, a hue is at its most intense. When a hue is muted or gray (that is, when its complementary color or gray or black has been added) it is less saturated.

Hues that contain white are known as tints. When we add white to pure hues they become lighter. Tints appear more alive and reflect more light than spectrum colors or

This is an example of using a fully saturated color, deep orange, to produce a rich effect, ideal for formal social events. Saturated hues can be combined with their complementary colors, such as orange with blue, to create a vibrant color scheme.

Here, a little white has been added to lighten the orange and create a warm, summery, and generally welcoming atmosphere, ideal for more informal social gatherings. The cream upholstery helps ensure that the overall effect is not too stimulating.

In this picture, much more white has been added to the orange to create a tint. By lightening the color of the background to this degree, the room now seems much more open and airy, suitable to be the main family room, and for general activities.

hues that contain black. Pink is a tint of red, while peach is a tint of orange. Tints are often called pastels or powder colors. And because they are easy on the eye, a space decorated with pastels is easy to live in, providing a backdrop for your changing moods.

A shade is a hue to which black has been added, making it appear darker than the spectrum color from which it is derived. This can make a dramatic change. For example, adding black to red will turn it into maroon, while a shade of yellow will become brown.

Deep saturation allows the hue's natural intensity and qualities to be used to maximum effect. Here, the deep indigo of the walls creates a cocooned space that feels warming, intimate, and secure—a haven on cold winter evenings.

More gray and some white has been added to the pure hue to create a cooler, more subtle tone that is less vibrant and imposing. The room now seems more coolly reflective, a suitable venue for activities such as light reading or study.

The more gray you add, the more muted and neutral the color becomes, creating a more subtle and less distinctive mood. The room appears both relaxing and inspiring, a place to recharge the batteries while planning the day ahead.

hues and **tones**

color palette

The tone of a color describes its value, brilliance, and luminosity. Hues mixed with gray are often referred to as tones, and can be muted and dusky as they are less bright than the spectrum colors. A tone can be either light or dark depending on whether black has been added to a light color or white to a dark color. Degree of tone also has a role to play.

Choosing the right tone is therefore as important as selecting the right hue.

We tend to think of a color as just one tone, whereas a single color can often reflect more than one wavelength of light, giving it an iridescent quality like that of a peacock's feather or mother-of-pearl shell. The color showing through is known as an undertone.

above Muted tones can be light or dark but give a more subtle and sophisticated effect. Here, a light tone creates a more spacious and airy feel.

above This lemon yellow has been lightened with the addition of some white but still has good saturation that creates a definite statement.

right Dark, fully saturated tones have the most brilliance and intensity and so make the most impact, enhancing the special qualities of the color.

color **temperature**

A color can be hot or cold in tone—referred to as its temperature. Red-orange provides the greatest sense of warmth, whereas blue-green gives us the greatest sense of cold. The temperature of a color is also relative because although blue is essentially a cold color, some blues are warmer than others.

The temperature of a color can also be affected by its undertone and whether a hue has a warm or cool look. Every color can be regarded as either hot or cold depending on its undertone. So, for example, even though we think of red as being a hot color, it may well have a cool undertone.

below Color temperatures can be fine-tuned by adjusting their value from light to dark to suit the mood you require and the conditions in the room.

VALUE AND TRANSPARENCY

Value describes how light or dark a color appears relative to black or white. Therefore, the value of a dark yellow might be the equivalent of a medium to light value of blue.

The thickness of the pigment or dye indicates its opacity or transparency. Opaque paints cover up any previous layers, while transparent pigments (such as colorwashes, which are thin films of pigment sometimes used on walls but most often on furniture to produce a distressed look) have the ability to transmit light and allow previous color layers to show through. So if a transparent red is applied over a transparent blue, or vice versa, the color will appear violet.

above Red is the hottest color and blue is the coolest, but temperature varies within each color range. From an observer's perspective, warm colors tend to advance so that the wall looks nearer. Cool colors recede and create the illusion of more space.

Choosing colors that work well together is not always easy. For example, if you use too few colors, a room can look cold and dull, while too many colors can make it appear loud and messy. There are those who

balance so that the colors you use look harmonious and pleasing.

A color wheel can help you to achieve a balanced scheme in a number of ways, as shown in the color combinations in the panel

color **harmonies**

Like musical notes, some colors combine to create perfect harmonies while other combinations seem discordant. A few simple rules can keep you in tune.

have an almost natural ability to coordinate colors well, but if you aren't one of these people, you can learn how to combine colors by following some simple rules of color harmony. The overall aim is to find the right

below. The first two harmonies create interiors that are comfortable and relaxing to live with, while the second two methods ensure that your environment is more stimulating and exciting.

MONOCHROMATIC HARMONY

A color scheme based on one color is known as a monochromatic harmony, and is often found in nature. For example, we see it in the varying shades of green leaves or the different blues of the sea. If you are uncertain as to what color to use for a monochromatic scheme, go for one that complements your existing furniture and make sure that you vary the tones from very light to very dark. Select lighter tones for areas where you need to reflect light, such as on the walls, and use darker, more intense hues for accent colors—that is, tones that set off your main color(s), such as in furnishings and accessories. In addition, neutrals work well as monochromatic schemes.

ADJACENT HARMONY

This is a color harmony made up of related hues that are adjacent on the color wheel. As they belong to the same family of colors, they look good next to each other in a color scheme. However, color schemes based on similar colors can sometimes look unbalanced. To avoid a room appearing too hot or too cold, too bright or too intense, you should include different tones and color intensities to break up the similar colors. For example, a warm color scheme of red, orange, and yellow would be more successful if cream was used on the walls, and russet and deep red reserved for the furnishings. Touches of a contrasting color should also be added to set off your chosen color family and bring the scheme to life.

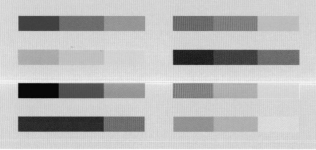

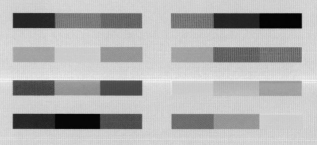

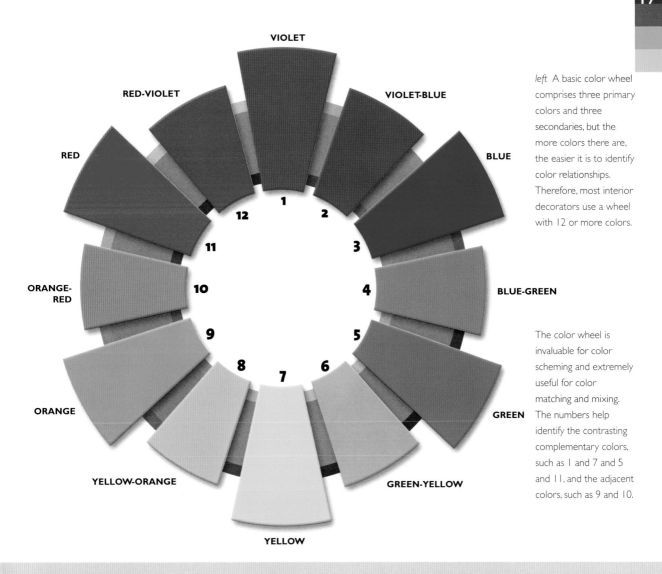

VIOLET

RED-VIOLET

VIOLET-BLUE

RED

BLUE

1
12
2
11
3
10
4
9
5
8 7 6

BLUE-GREEN

ORANGE-RED

ORANGE

GREEN

YELLOW-ORANGE

GREEN-YELLOW

YELLOW

left A basic color wheel comprises three primary colors and three secondaries, but the more colors there are, the easier it is to identify color relationships. Therefore, most interior decorators use a wheel with 12 or more colors.

The color wheel is invaluable for color scheming and extremely useful for color matching and mixing. The numbers help identify the contrasting complementary colors, such as 1 and 7 and 5 and 11, and the adjacent colors, such as 9 and 10.

CONTRAST HARMONY

This form of harmony instills vitality and life into a basic color scheme by introducing touches of strong contrasting colors. For example, a contrasting accent color could be introduced into a monochromatic scheme so that it brings much-needed excitement and drama into an otherwise neutral environment. Alternatively, touches of a contrasting color could be introduced into an adjacent scheme; for example, a bedroom decorated in creamy yellow and terracotta could be given a boost by adding touches of purple. Accents of contrasting colors need not be limited to areas of paintwork, but can also be included in the furnishings, artwork, ornaments, and even in the choice of houseplants.

COMPLEMENTARY HARMONY

This is another form of contrasting harmony, one that uses the complementary color as accent to the main color scheme, whether this is one color or a family of colors. Complementary harmony is the most dramatic of all color scheming as it uses the natural intensity of contrasting complementary hues. While complementary colors create an exciting and intense atmosphere, take care when using two colors of the same intensity as this can create a strobe effect that can be very unnerving and uncomfortable. The solution is either to separate the colors with neutrals or tone down one of the complementary colors so that it is lighter or darker than the other.

color **harmonies** continued

COLOR SCHEMES FOR LIFESTYLES

Often we have fixed ideas about color schemes. Sometimes we repeat colors that we have lived with before in other homes, or we may wish to copy exactly a room we have seen in a book or magazine. However, color schemes that look good in a picture or showroom are often staged and so do not take into account the practicalities of everyday life. In addition, colors that look good in other people's homes would not necessarily look good in ours.

It is therefore important to make sure that you really like the colors you have seen elsewhere and that they would really enhance your lifestyle. For example, a minimalist look may be just the thing for a person who leads a hectic life, but for a homely individual or a family with small children this style may be impractical. On similar lines, while dramatic colors can be inspirational for a strong personality, they would not suit someone who prefers a quiet and simple way of life.

right Red, yellow, and blue are the primary colors and these make a bold statement on the walls and fabrics in this living room. This color scheme suits a dynamic, expressive type but might overwhelm a more reclusive individual.

left Orange is a breezy, sociable color for fun-loving, party-going types, but it can be too energetic for everyday living unless harmonized with more muted tones, as shown here.

DECIDING ON A COLOR

One way of deciding whether colors are right for you is to consider carefully what your expectations are for your home. When choosing colors to suit your lifestyle, remember that the rules of color harmony still apply. For example, if you envisage your home as:

■ a peaceful retreat: use soft colors with plenty of green.

■ a party house: use hot, bright, dramatic colors.

■ a creative haven: use a mix of your favorite colors and unusual combinations.

■ a place to relax: use neutral and light tones.

■ a busy family home: use warm hues for living areas and cool colors for private spaces.

■ an exotic paradise: use a combination of deep, rich colors.

■ an esthetic masterpiece: use muted tones and a restricted palette.

The colors we choose for our home offer an important means of self-expression. They tell us who we are and reflect our attitudes and lifestyles. Having colors around us that convey our personality makes us feel relaxed and so brings out the best in us.

We are all attracted to things that mirror something in ourselves, and similar characteristics can be found in our choice of friends, partners, and even our pets. In the same way, when you walk around a house, the colors you find will reveal a great deal about the

color **personality**

The colors we choose to decorate the home not only provide a true reflection of our inner selves but also say much about the type of people we like to mix with.

RED

1 Red is bold and energetic. People who like red are strong, dynamic, and physically active. They like to be in control of events and get things done.

2 The red personality is always on the go and may find it difficult to sit down and relax for any length of time without looking for a task to perform.

3 Red shows a need to feel secure and protected. It suggests a household where the occupants have lots of different interests and routines, who regularly like to go out to socialize and who enjoy travel.

4 The red personality enjoys adventure and taking risks. This will be reflected in the bold use of colors and the style of paintings and ornaments on display.

ORANGE

1 Orange is an uplifting and lively color, reflecting a household where there is plenty of fun and where popular social functions are held often.

2 A love of orange represents a person who is cheerful and loves sensory pleasures, someone who likes to share time and communicate with others, while enjoying a delicious home-cooked meal.

3 Homes decorated predominantly in tones of orange or brown suggest a very practical attitude to life that revolves around the home and family.

4 The orange personality does not favor solitude. A home decorated in this color shows a desire for companionship and a talent for making friends.

people who live there. Much depends on who has chosen the colors. If only one member of the family has decided on the color scheme, it is more than likely that he or she will have selected the hues that reflect his or her own personality, rather than those of a partner, family member, or roommate.

If this person has a dominant personality, these colors may leave the other members of the household feeling uncomfortable and withdrawn, so it is important that everyone in the home likes the colors used in shared spaces, with personal preferences reserved for private areas and rooms used only by a particular member of the household.

COLORS HAVE PERSONALITIES TOO

Not only can we use color as a language to express who we are, but colors also have their own distinctive personalities. These are based on their universal qualities and also on our personal and cultural associations with each

YELLOW

1 Yellow is a bright happy color and the most visible of all the colors.

2 A love of yellow shows someone with a clever and optimistic disposition, who has many different interests, and is sociable and lively.

3 Yellow is the color of the mind and intellect. Golden tones reflect a person full of ideas and who is good at communicating these thoughts to others.

4 Homes decorated in yellow suggest a desire for a happy and healthy lifestyle. This color fits well with the quest for regular exercise—especially outdoor activities, often involving large groups of friends—healthy, natural food, and mental stimulation.

BLUE

1 Blue has an introverted personality and fits well with those who have a love of peace and quiet.

2 People who favor blue may prefer intellectual or creative pursuits such as reading, music, and art, or they may work with others as teachers or healers.

3 Blue suggests a calm and quiet atmosphere where everyone is able to get on with their particular interests in peace and without disruption.

4 Homes decorated predominantly in blues show a preference for solitude, and a desire to create a private haven away from the stresses of modern life.

color **personality** continued

color. These color associations are powerful. When we see a color it triggers the thoughts and feelings that have developed through our past experiences, both good and bad.

However, psychologists have found that our reactions to many of the colors in our surroundings are similar. For example, looking into the blue sky is a calming, relaxing experience for most people, while we find red, the color of blood and fire, bold and attention-grabbing. Similarly, it has been found that our responses are very much alike when we are

BLACK AND WHITE

1 A home decorated in strong, contrasting neutrals reflects a personality that needs to be ordered, or perhaps a desire to maintain control.

2 This choice of hues suggests a personality who may wish to simplify his or her life and go back to basics.

3 Occupants of homes decorated in strong contrasts such as black and white are often single-minded and may be following a specific path in life.

4 Simple schemes based on black and white often show a quest for simplicity and purity—an antidote to the modern world of neon and technicolor.

5 Black-and-white contrasts can indicate a more spiritual outlook, as seen in the Japanese minimalist style. This tends to emphasize shape and texture, especially of natural objects, rather than colors.

PINK

1 Although pink is a tint of red, it has a very distinct color personality all of its own.

2 While red is the color of the passion and physicality of love, pink reflects its softer, more romantic side.

3 Often, we are drawn to candy or baby pink when we are going through a difficult time emotionally. In this case, we are using the language of color as a cry for help by seeking the security of infancy.

4 For some people, pink symbolizes their loving and nurturing nature and they are happy to reveal this fact by decorating their homes in pink.

5 Deep pinks reflect the more sensual side of a person and so may be reserved for the bedroom. Lighter tones are often chosen by compassionate souls who work for the good of others.

placed in rooms decorated with specific colors: in an orange room we are more likely to talk to one another and move around, while in a blue room most people stay quiet and seated.

So the personality of a color can be a guide to where to use it in your home, as different colors can alter the way you respond and use a room. If you want to feel more sociable and communicative, you might introduce orange and yellow tones. If you prefer a quieter life, include some calming blue or green. Incorporating objects that symbolize particular colors is a good way of bringing positive associations into your home.

VIOLET

1 A preference for violet indicates a creative and unconventional personality, someone seeking personal development by exploring a more spiritual path or through creative expression.

2 Violet is most strongly associated with the emperors of ancient Rome. A strong use of violet in a home can show a love of luxury and drama.

3 Though a love of violet expresses a resilient and powerful personality, it may also show a need to feel special and to stand out from the crowd.

4 Violet may also suggest a person who needs to make a visible statement about him- or herself, and to ensure that he or she does not go unnoticed.

5 People who favor violet may not be the easiest to get along with but they also ensure that time spent in their presence is not easily forgotten.

NEUTRALS

1 A love of neutrals reveals an independent person who prefers to lead life away from the limelight.

2 Neutrals provide a blank canvas that allows flexibility of living. They are favored by people who don't like to be pinned down, or who may be going through life changes, and don't want to commit themselves to one particular style.

If using neutrals to highlight other colors, look at the meanings of these other colors too.

GREEN

1 Green has a relaxed, easygoing personality and reflects a love of nature and a healthy lifestyle. It may indicate an animal lover, a gardener, or someone interested in the healing arts.

2 Homes decorated in green demonstrate a desire for calm and to create a peaceful retreat. The green personality may find it difficult to make decisions and often leaves color choices to someone else.

color **personality** continued

A color's highly individual personality can transform a room. When choosing the main room color, you need to take into account not only your personality and preferences but also whether the personality of the color is appropriate for the use to which that room will be put. Outlines of the personalities of six colors are given below, together with pictures

Red has a strong, vibrant personality. It is the color of blood, fire, and passion, and is symbolic of life itself. We associate this color with action and vigor and often with anger and aggression. Throughout history, red has been closely linked with acts of violence and also death. At the same time, this eye-catching color is also the color of love and happiness.

Orange has a creative, fun-loving personality. It is a striking color that we associate with harvest time and the colors of fruits and flowers, and with strong scents and tastes. When we think of orange, ripe peaches and squashes, late-summer flowers, and amber honey come to mind, so orange has strong sensory connections and a built-in feel-good factor.

Yellow has a bright, alert personality. Golden yellow is symbolic of the sun with all its power and life-giving energy, reminding us of idyllic vacations. In daylight we feel safe, alert, and active, and so we think of yellow as a warm, friendly color. Yet we see green-yellow as decay in nature and so associate negative emotions such as jealousy and cowardice with these hues.

of the same room decorated in those colors. You will notice how the choice of color changes the mood of the room. Try to avoid tones with which you may have formed undesirable associations. Also, like everything in life, an excess can change a positive into negative, so it is wise not to use too much of any one color in your home.

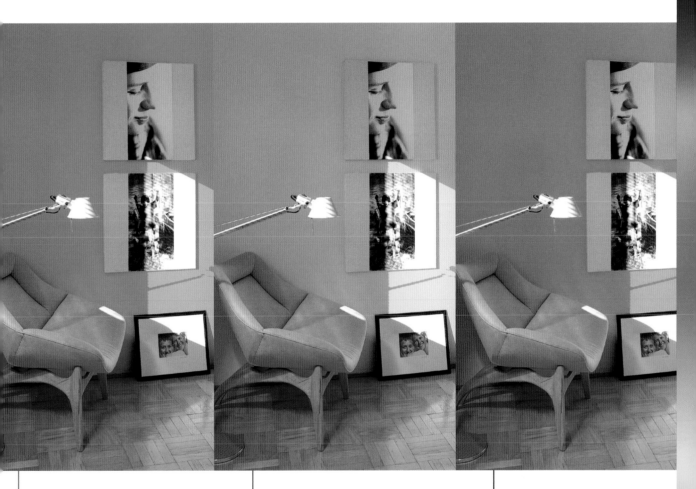

Green has a harmonious, restful personality. It is the color of the plant kingdom, and the natural world in general, and suggests balance and harmony on earth. Spring greens are linked to growth and youthfulness, and create a light, airy mood in a room, while darker greens are more lush and mysterious and make a much bolder statement.

Blue has a quiet, soothing personality. We usually imagine the vast expanse of the sky and the universe when we experience blue, so it is a contemplative color. Darker shades have deeper and more mysterious associations, for example with the sky at midnight and the vastness of the oceans. For these reasons, blue has a strong connection with sleep and dreaming.

Violet has a dramatic, mysterious personality, and this is reflected in the symbolism of this color in many religions and is reinforced by its appearance in nature. Sparkling minerals such as amethysts, and the patterns found in the iridescent plumage of some birds and on the wings of butterflies, make violet a color of surprise and wonder.

Nature is constantly changing, and each season brings with it a varying array of beautiful colors that project the appropriate kind of energy for the particular time of year.

we work in harmony with nature, the changing proportions of the spectrum colors in daylight act on our psyche to harmonize our body clocks and biorhythms so that we are better able to pace ourselves throughout the

seasonal color

By making use of the changing colors of the seasons, we enjoy the health-giving benefits that accrue from being in tune with the annual cycles of nature.

If you live in the countryside, you will be naturally connected to the changing seasons, but even if you live in town, your life can be enriched by honoring seasonal colors. When

year. Creating a link between our home and the colors of the seasons can have a positive effect on our moods and outlook, and can help to keep us in high spirits.

COLORS AND HEALTH

Each spectrum color has unique qualities that affect specific organs, glands, and systems in the body. Light therapists believe we should seek out those hues that have positive health benefits and avoid any colors that may cause imbalances and lead to mental and physical illness if left uncorrected.

RED
stimulates body functions, accelerating the heartbeat and pulse, and causing the release of adrenaline into the bloodstream and an increase in muscle tension.

YELLOW
affects our nervous system and the workings of the liver, gallbladder, and pancreas. It also stimulates the mind and makes us feel more alert.

BLUE
depresses all our bodily functions so that we slow down; it also affects the workings of the thyroid and thymus glands, as well as our ears, throat, and eyes.

ORANGE
stimulates our appetite and digestive system, and boosts the body's immune system, so helping to strengthen our resistance to infections and other diseases.

GREEN
affects our respiratory system and acts on the parasympathetic nervous system. This has a calming and relaxing effect and so helps to combat stress.

VIOLET
affects our head, spine, and central nervous system. It also affects our psyche and helps balance the left- and right-hand brain to boost reasoning and intuitive skills.

SEASONAL COLORS

SPRING COLORS (soft white, pale pink, light blue, lilac, cream, and pale green) are soft, muted, and light, redolent of new shoots, vibrant plant growth, delicate blossoms, and clear morning skies.

SUMMER COLORS (sky blue, grass green, golden yellow, orange, peach, cream, mango, scarlet, turquoise, and white) are clear, bright hues and bright primaries suggesting sand and sunny skies.

FALL COLORS (crimson, ocher, rust, nut, mahogany, deep blue, indigo, and violet) are warm and rich shades with a yellow-gold undertone reflecting golds, oranges, yellows, and earth browns.

WINTER COLORS (white, black, ice-blue, silver, gold, dark green, burgundy, magenta, and fuchsia) are deep and strongly contrasted, evoking a leaden sky, snow-covered rocks, and skiing vacations.

color palette

right Spring colors are light blues and bright yellows. Pastel hues on the walls help reflect the maximum amount of light into the room.

spring **color**

As well as its own colors, each season has its own feeling and atmosphere that we can bring into our home.

Spring is the time of renewal and cleansing. After the long dark days of winter, spring light is crisp and clear. The first snowdrops appear and early spring flowers reflect pale tints and soft pinks and creams in order to make the most of the lower light levels. If you have used wintertime to renew your energy and plan ahead, in spring you will naturally start to feel restless and begin to look forward to making a new start.

This is the perfect time to purge and to spring-clean your home. Remove clutter from window sills and clean window panes to let in as much daylight as possible. To refresh your home even further, replace darker-toned blankets, throws, rugs, and cushions with lighter, paler hues.

summer **color**

Nature celebrates summer with a riot of wonderful bright colors. Flowers are rich and vivid, and the greens of the grass and trees reach a deep intensity. This is the time when we are naturally most physically active and when our energy levels are high.

Bringing a variety of bright colors into your home during the summer will help you celebrate who you are and sustain your enthusiasm for life. Take time to experiment and put your plans into action. This is a good season to change your color scheme and to tackle building or refurbishment work.

Fill your home with bowls of colorful flowers or architectural plants, and make the most of the longer days by turning your attention to making any outdoor spaces and entertainment areas more colorful too.

left Summer colors are bright and sunny. Sky blue walls provide a natural backdrop to foliage-rich houseplants.

color palette

fall **color**

color palette

As summer passes, the rich, deep shades of fall come to the fore. Trees are clothed in changing tones of gold, red, and copper, and many fruits and berries ripen to deep blue and violet. At this time of harvesting, nature draws in energy in preparation for the winter months. During fall, we should start to slow down our physical activities and gather our strength for the winter season. It is a good time to think about making your home as comfortable and nurturing as possible, perhaps with replacement furniture and furnishings. You can also introduce the colors of fall in a bowl of harvest fruit and decorative vegetables such as squashes.

In order to make your home more snug and inviting, introduce richer, deeper colors that will create winter cheer. However, while tones should remain warm to keep energy levels high, it is a good idea to also include cooler tones to help you slow down. Purple, violet, and rich magenta all contain both warming red and soothing blue, making them perfect choices for the time of year.

right Fall colors are rich and earthy, reflecting russet leaves and ripe fruit to create a warm and cozy feel.

left Winter colors feature strong contrasts and shiny surfaces to make the most of the light from the waning sun and encourage a mood of introspection.

winter **color**

When winter comes we should be well prepared to spend a few months indoors. Nature is at rest and takes time to renew its energy before the next cycle begins. We should also use our time in more reflective pursuits, replenishing our energy levels and taking stock of our lives. This is a good time to plan your color schemes, ready to put them into action in the new year.

The short, dark days at this time of year naturally make us crave warmth and mental stimulation, so rich, warm colors can really help us through the winter months. We need to feel snug and relaxed and to take time to entertain our family and friends. Winter is also a time of celebration, so light-reflecting colors such as silver, gold, and metallic finishes bring some sparkle into our lives during the otherwise gloomier months.

These colors can be used as decorative accents in cushions and candles, and table and mantel decorations, and beds can be dressed in deeper, richer colors that create a sense of warmth and mystery; all of which can easily be removed when the next cycle begins and springtime calls for change.

color palette

Nature is a wonderful decorator, mixing and matching colors to perfection. Although its color schemes may appear haphazard, often the strong, contrasting hues have a clear purpose. For example, glance, natural objects tend to appear to be one color, but when you look at them carefully in natural light, it soon becomes apparent that they are composed of a variety of subtle hues. Pebbles and shells are made up of several

inspiration from **nature**

Looking at the perfect way nature uses harmonies and contrasts shows us how to combine colors in the home in a balanced and harmonious way.

The way individual hues appear in nature can give us a clue as to how colors affect space and the best way to use them in the home, as described below.

many flowers display striking colors in order to attract pollinating birds or insects.

Some species of insects, birds, and animals use several colors to harmonize with the landscape as a means of camouflage. At first harmonizing colors, or tones of the same color, which has a gentle, relaxing effect on the eye. When we copy nature's color schemes, we can be sure to achieve in our homes the same effects as those of the natural world.

NATURE'S COLORS IN THE HOME

RED

Red is the color of blood and fire, and so is associated with heat and vitality. We find many beautiful tones of red in the earth, and when we use these in our homes we get a sense of grounding and security.

Red is often a transitory color: like fire it moves and changes. We may see it in the sky at sunset or in a field of poppies. So we can use this quality of red in home decorating to encourage a sense of movement through a space. Red makes a room appear smaller, and so it may have a claustrophobic effect, but it comes into its own when set against cool colors.

ORANGE

Orange is the color of the sunset, harvest vegetables, and falling leaves. It brings a sense of satisfaction similar to the feeling you get after a good meal. Tones of orange have been found to affect us both physically and psychologically, by stimulating the appetite and bringing a feeling of comfort and contentment.

A bright orange has warming qualities. It makes a room appear smaller, and yet it is much less oppressive than red. Orange is best used to decorate welcoming parts of the home, such as dining areas and those places where we need to feel both relaxed and emotionally supported.

YELLOW

This is the color most often associated with the sun and with summer outdoor activities. Many sun-loving flowers are golden yellow, and when we look at yellow we feel alive, awake, and mentally uplifted. In the home, a vibrant splash of yellow can bring the strength and vitality of sunlight into a cold, dull space.

Though yellow does not have the ability to make a room look larger, its atmosphere of warmth and cheerfulness means that it is a popular choice to brighten small rooms. Yellow ocher is a darker color and so is better suited to larger spaces, or to create a strong sense of security.

GREEN

A green landscape comprises many different tones, from the pale yellow-green of new shoots to the deep, bluish-black shades of large trees. In our homes, too, green looks much better when we mimic this layered effect.

A large, flat expanse of green on walls looks dull and lifeless, but when greens are placed with contrasting colors or several different tones of green are used together, it creates a relaxing haven without being soporific. Green works well if introduced into patterns in your furnishings, and, as in nature, it can make a wonderful background color for more contrasting hues.

COLORS IN LANDSCAPES

A good way of taking inspiration from nature is to look at the colors in landscapes, where different shapes, hues, and textures combine to create a mood. If you can't get to the seaside, countryside, or mountains, study vacation brochures, calendars, or magazines.

Looking at the landscape as a whole, rather than at just one object, will give you a color palette, and when used together in your home these tones can affect your mood as if you were experiencing the actual place.

For example, the bright, warm colors of the sun and sand bring a feeling of joy and movement to your home, while cool blues and white create a mood that is fresh and invigorating. Sky blue and soft pastels re-create the sense of fresh mountain air and alpine flowers in a mountain meadow. Rich, warm harmonies of reds, golds, and browns reflect the protective atmosphere of a forest in fall.

Natural landscapes don't have to be places you have actually visited, just places that stimulate your imagination or that you find interesting and mysterious. Look at a picture of an underwater scene and you will find a completely different range of colors from those on land, and a night sky or a picture taken from space create different atmospheres from the landscapes you know.

BLUE

Blue is usually associated with the vast expanses of the sea and sky. Our eyes find blue soothing, and when we look at large areas of this color, our minds enter a sense of deep relaxation and we feel calm and peaceful. Pale blue tints make an interior space feel light and airy, while deeper tones of blue are more relaxing and give an atmosphere of mystery.

Deep blue and indigo reflect little light and can be depressing when used on their own, and so are better kept as accent colors in private spaces, especially for contemplation. They also promote deeper sleep, so you can retreat into your dreamtime.

VIOLET

Violet is a dramatic color that is not often found in nature, and so it fills us with a sense of mystery and surprise when it does appear. For example, it is always exciting when a mountain takes on a violet hue at sunset, or when we get a hint of deep violet while looking into the vast ocean.

Violet is also an eye-catching color. We are naturally drawn to a violet flower or a gemstone that reflects violet light. In our homes, we can maintain this element of surprise and reinforce the effects of such an exotic and luxurious color by taking care to use it sparingly in places where it will have most dramatic effect.

WHITE

There is no true white in nature. Objects we think of as white are pale tints of another color. White flowers are very pale blue, lilac, or pink, and white stones are likely to be a pale blue, tan, or gray. Brilliant-white paint contains zinc, which prevents light from being absorbed by the pigment, thus reflecting all the colors to create the illusion of a bright white.

Large expanses of white reflect too much light and this glare can overstimulate the nervous system, making us feel tired and irritable. It is better to take a tip from nature and use off-white or the palest tints to complement the rest of your color scheme.

BLACK

Like white, pure black is rarely found in nature. The night sky is a deep, midnight blue, and black rocks and stones often have violet or brown undertones; so if you decide to use black paint, it is better to make it with warm or cool undertones by mixing other color paints together. If you want to enjoy the true beauty of black, incorporate it in the natural materials around your home. Pure black seams appear in some types of granite and marble. A slate floor or marble work surface will add depth to your color scheme and will provide accent coloring to highlight other shades.

color **check-up**

Changing a color scheme can be a daunting task and very often people live with colors they do not like for fear of trying something new. If moving into a new residence, it is a good idea to wait until you know your home better before painting the rooms. If you want to redecorate your existing home, it can be helpful to assess which areas need a facelift. To avoid the process becoming a hit-and-miss affair, there are lots of things to consider before choosing a color scheme.

First you need to pick your main color(s) and decide whether or not you will use a monochromatic scheme. If you select two or

ROOM CHECK-UP

This first part of the room check-up helps you assess your feelings about your existing home and determine which rooms need attention. Walk around your home and answer the following questions for each room.

HOW DOES THE ROOM LOOK NOW? (TICK THE BOTTOM BOX IF YOU WOULD LIKE TO CHANGE THE LOOK OR STYLE.)

LOOK	HALL	LIVING ROOM	DINING ROOM	KITCHEN
FRESH AND CLEAN				
OUTDATED				
STYLISH AND ATTRACTIVE				
DARK AND DREARY				
BRIGHT AND AIRY				
HOT AND STUFFY				
COMFORTABLE AND HOMELY				
WORN AND SHABBY				
MESSY AND CLUTTERED				
ORDERLY AND WELL-PLANNED				
CHANGE				

Now sit quietly in the room and focus on the way it makes you feel. Ask yourself whether this feeling is appropriate to the room or whether you need to change the mood, and then write down the mood you wish to create.

FEELING	HALL	LIVING ROOM	DINING ROOM	KITCHEN	
BORED					
RELAXED					
IRRITABLE					
INSPIRED					
ENERGETIC					
SLEEPY					
WELCOME					
DEPRESSED					
COMFORTABLE					
DESIRED MOOD					

more colors, you will need to find the best combinations of these. Once you have established which areas need new colors you will also have to determine whether you are going to introduce seasonal or new accent colors, or completely redecorate.

If you are not used to color scheming, it is a good idea to start redecorating the smaller and less-used areas, such as a spare room, hall, or stairs. Once you have created a new look that you are pleased with, you will have the confidence to tackle the main living areas. Working through a checklist can help you decide what is the best scheme so that you don't have to redecorate several times before finding the right combination.

BATHROOM	STUDY/DEN	BED 1	BED 2	BED 3

BATHROOM	STUDY/DEN	BED 1	BED 2	BED 3

ARE YOU HAPPY WITH HOW YOU USE THE SPACE?	YES	NO	CHANGE TO
HALL			
LIVING ROOM			
DINING ROOM			
KITCHEN			
BATHROOM			
STUDY/DEN			
BEDROOM 1			
BEDROOM 2			
BEDROOM 3			
OTHER AREAS			

color **check-up** continued

This part will help you decide which colors to use in your scheme. Look at the checklists you have completed to see which rooms need redecorating, and then ask yourself whether you need to change the look, the style, the mood, or the way you use the space.

CHANGING THE LOOK OR STYLE

Color is a wonderful way to change the look of a room with instant results. By painting the walls or adding accent colors, you can transform a cold, dark room into a bright, attractive space, or make a large, cold area snug and welcoming.

To make a room appear:

- larger: use light tints and neutrals.
- smaller: use rich or darker shades or a bright accent color on one wall.
- multifunctional: use neutrals with accent colors in different areas.
- brighter: use bright, warm colors.
- airy and spacious: use light colors, neutrals, and pastels.
- uncluttered: use just one or two colors in a room.
- warm and welcoming: use rich, warm tones.
- cozy: use deep, hot colors.
- fresh and clean: use clear, light colors.

If your room looks outdated and shabby, you may want to change the style. This usually entails modifying or replacing some or all of the furniture and furnishings, and also the floor coverings, and not just changing the color scheme. You will need to decide which style or period you wish to create and then choose the colors that reflect that particular style.

CHANGING THE MOOD

If you want to make your home feel more:

- welcoming: use some warm, earthy colors.
- relaxing: make it more neutral or add some cool, light colors.
- soothing: add some light blue, light green, or rose pink.
- sociable: pep up the space with rich, warm colors like peach, gold, orange, and red.
- stimulating: decorate in bright, hot color harmonies.
- calming: use cool harmonies such as deeper blue and rich green.
- romantic: add soft pink, green, mauve, lilac, or faded tones.
- dramatic: use strong contrasts or complementary hues.
- vibrant: use rich, warm colors and triadic tones.
- sensual: use warm harmonies of reds, pinks, mauves, and purples.
- sophisticated: use neutrals and muted tones.

CHANGING THE USE

You may need to carry out some structural changes to achieve this, but adapting or replacing the furniture and choosing colors to suit the activities you wish to do in the space can sometimes be enough to change the way you use a room. If you wish to change the look of the room, ask yourself how this can best be accomplished. Once you have decided on the change of focus, you need to choose your new main color(s) and accent colors.

COLOR TRENDS

Decorating entirely according to the latest trends can prove a disaster if the colors you use do not suit your home and lifestyle. If it is important to you that your color scheme is fashionable, looking through magazines and visiting decorating and home stores can help you find trendy colors and furnishings that appeal to you. These days there is never just one trend, and so you should be able to find several color schemes that look contemporary, yet still express your particular personality and lifestyle, and the style of your home.

Inspiration for your main color(s) can come from:

- your favorite color or color personality.
- a special painting, rug, vase, or piece of furniture.
- a natural object.
- a specific style such as country, modern, or classic.
- the shape and orientation of the room.
- the specific mood or feeling you want to achieve.

Accent colors are tones that complement and set-off your main color(s). They can be a permanent part of your color scheme, such as on woodwork, doors, windows, or furnishings and drapes. However, accent colors can also be changeable and you can add them to suit your different moods or to create seasonal harmony. Houseplants offer an easy and effective way to provide temporary accent colors through the careful choice of foliage and blooms to complement your decor. You can make major changes simply by moving plants to different locations within a room, or to different rooms. Similarly, by choosing ornaments, paintings, or even coffee table books in accent colors you can create a pleasingly coordinated effect for the minimum effort. Take care to ensure that the style of art you choose, and not just the predominant colors, fits in with the overall scheme.

Fill in these room color schemes to see at a glance what colors, moods, and themes you will use. They will help you create continuity and good color contrasts between rooms.

HALL AND STAIRS

I am happy with this room	
Change use to	
Change look to	
Change mood to	
Main color(s)	
Accent colors	

LIVING ROOM

I am happy with this room	
Change use to	
Change look to	
Change mood to	
Main color(s)	
Accent colors	

DINING ROOM

I am happy with this room	
Change use to	
Change look to	
Change mood to	
Main color(s)	
Accent colors	

KITCHEN

I am happy with this room	
Change use to	
Change look to	
Change mood to	
Main color(s)	
Accent colors	

BATHROOM

I am happy with this room	
Change use to	
Change look to	
Change mood to	
Main color(s)	
Accent colors	

STUDY/DEN

I am happy with this room	
Change use to	
Change look to	
Change mood to	
Main color(s)	
Accent colors	

BEDROOM 1

I am happy with this room	
Change use to	
Change look to	
Change mood to	
Main color(s)	
Accent colors	

BEDROOM 2

I am happy with this room	
Change use to	
Change look to	
Change mood to	
Main color(s)	
Accent colors	

BEDROOM 3

I am happy with this room	
Change use to	
Change look to	
Change mood to	
Main color(s)	
Accent colors	

BEDROOM 4

I am happy with this room	
Change use to	
Change look to	
Change mood to	
Main color(s)	
Accent colors	

the
red family

Red, orange, and yellow are the warriors of the color world, representing our lifeblood and the rich, warm tones of the earth. Red is the strongest and most vibrant of this family. Its warmth stimulates the body and mind, making us feel alert and alive. Red brings life and vitality to an interior space, and when we are surrounded by the grounding tones of red, orange, and gold we feel relaxed and secure. Bright and nurturing, these hues create a safe haven where we can laugh and talk. They are the family of communication, the sociable colors of the spectrum.

FOR OTHER SENSUAL OR
LUXURIOUS COLORS, SEE ALSO:

PASSION FLOWER **60**

EMERALD RICH **172**

THE SPIRIT OF VIOLET **184**

DEEP PURPLE **188**

Red is a mover and shaker and is not for the fainthearted. It represents our life energy—the blood. Its tones can be deep and rich or soft and warm, but whichever red you choose, it will tantalize the senses and stir make a room look smaller, while the lighter hues create a warm and cozy feel. When you use red on a single wall or ceiling, it will make this area appear closer to you, so it is useful for open-plan living rooms and in rooms with

the spirit of red

Red tones bring vibrancy and a dynamic quality to the home. They create movement and change, and bring life and vitality to an interior space.

color palette

your passions. Use it where you want to make a statement and encourage movement in your home. It will boost your energy levels and heighten your enthusiasm for life. The bold, dynamic personality of red makes it a favorite of people who lead active, outgoing lives, but not everyone feels comfortable with this degree of stimulation. Although it can be the ultimate feel-good factor, such a strong color can make some people feel oppressed and hemmed in. Either way, when you see red, you will have a definite reaction to it.

HOW RED AFFECTS YOUR ROOM

Red has many guises—from deep wine and crimson to soft, gentle pinks and lilacs. The stronger, rich tones of red absorb light and

high ceilings. Use red on its own to bring drama to a single area. Highlight one wall in a deep magenta or cherry red to catch the attention and draw you into a space. Red doesn't have to be old fashioned; a raspberry crush or orchid pink can make a statement that is modern, young, and vibrant.

RED HARMONIES

Combine red with other colors in the same family to create a bright, happy atmosphere.

Golden yellow reflects more light than red, especially if you use shiny surfaces and mirrored finishes. This combination is more lively and uplifting than an all-red room. Red combines well with cool colors to create a bright but more relaxed space. If you look closely into a

left In this kitchen, the vivid red alone would create too much heat to be bearable day to day. However, the overall effect is nicely cooled by the neutral surfaces and streamlined steel of the faucet, sink, and chair legs.

use red to

- create a warm welcome

- move people around a space

- bring warmth to a cold, dark room

- renew your home's energy and vitality

- heat up your sex life

- create a safe, enclosed space

right A splash of red on the chair provides a point of focus and adds an element of surprise in an otherwise neutral kitchen.

opposite Using a harmony of red, orange, and yellow creates a lively and energetic space. Here, touches of blue and green calm an otherwise hot color scheme.

fire, you will see that the flames reflect not only the warm colors, but also the blues and greens. So, on the one hand, fire is vibrant and energetic, but on the other it can be cool and relaxing. Contrast red with blue, or red with green, in a multifunctional living room where you want to create a sociable place that is ideal for entertaining but that also provides some-where to relax on your own.

DANGER SIGNALS

Red signals danger in the natural world, and in home decoration, too, you need to exercise caution. We all need the dynamic energy and love of life offered by red, but many people find an all-red room oppressive. Red has a very powerful effect on our moods, so avoid red if you are quick to lose your temper. People who are affected by a "red rage" or suffer from heart problems or hot flushes should avoid spending too much time in red rooms, especially dark red, which can overstimulate the system. Deep pink, magenta, or pale pink and lilac are good alternatives, evoking love and support.

Red is not always brash; it has its calm side too. The lighter versions of red are found in the pink range and these gentle colors are linked to romantic love rather than physical passion. Soft pinks offer emotional support and are physically relaxing. Most people instinctively use these loving vibrations in their bedrooms and other private spaces.

royal **welcome**

FOR OTHER VIBRANT OR BOLD
COLORS, SEE ALSO:

THE SPIRIT OF YELLOW **92**

SHARP CONTRASTS **222**

The richness and vibrancy of the red family sets the perfect scene for making you feel welcome. Our first impression of a house is often the most lasting. It is the atmosphere of a hallway that gives a real royal welcome, making you feel honored and special. The entrance to your home is where you "touch base," so an alluring hallway decorated with rich, vibrant tones can really make you feel happy to be home. In addition, the grounding effect of red helps you to forget the stresses and strains of the outside world and soon brings you down to earth.

Your royal welcome can be more effective if you choose decor and furnishings that give a feeling of wealth, history, and tradition. A natural wood or tile floor in warm, earthy tones enhances the glow of traditional furniture, rich furnishings, and gilt-framed mirrors and paintings. In a period home it is better to

right Royal red, soothing white, ample light, and earthly neutrals make for a dreamy combination that is at once solid yet ethereal, comforting yet airy.

left The glossy
reflections from the
timber floor lead
the eye to the inner
rooms and bring life to
a dark corridor.

color palette

left A simple expanse of red is enough to make you feel welcome and entice you to sit down and relax in a large room.

right Strong contrasts of rich plum and brilliant white are eye-catching and create a cocooned but sophisticated place to relax.

steer clear of sharp contrasts of colors as these create a "spark" that cancels out the ideals of tradition and stability. Rather, it is better to combine red with gold, deep blue, and purple, which not only have royal associations but are also more relaxing.

A stairway is like the spine of the home, lending support to the upper floors. Deep warm shades act as foundation colors and can lift the atmosphere in a badly lit and dreary stairwell. A red wall can literally stop you in your tracks as you enter, giving you time to adjust to being inside, while a deep-red stair carpet will look rich and luxurious. White woodwork provides a good contrast if walls are decorated in deep warm tones, but

below By accentuating the enclosed space below stairs with deep tones, the staircase is not just given extra strength—it also seems to float upward.

right The bold use of
deep red around the
doorway creates a
strong, protected space
and also contrasts well
with the light streaming
through the frosted
glass doors.

opposite A luxurious
red carpet is a
dramatic feature that
promises secret
delights upstairs.

if lighter tints are used for the walls, a rich wooden staircase or rich brown-colored flooring will lend weight to the hall and stairs.

Another way to introduce red into the hallway of a period home is through stained-glass panels in the door or entranceway, which cause a changing pattern of light to fall onto the walls and floors within. A lighter wall color shows off this type of feature well, and if you have good lighting in the hallway the colored glass will look wonderful from the outside of the house at night.

red **cocoon**

When it's dark or cold, most people wish they were curled up on a comfy sofa in front of a roaring fire. Dancing flames have a magnetic quality that draws you in and makes you feel relaxed and secure. A snug haven can provide the perfect place to relax in the evening or on a winter's day, and even if the room does not have an open hearth, the same wonderful feeling can be created with color. Deep, warm tones will envelop you the minute you step inside, making you forget the world outside and transporting you to your own private place.

The beauty of a TV room is that it is best suited to a small space, even one located in a

cold or dark part of the house. Often these smaller rooms become cluttered or are simply neglected. However, if you have such a room in your house, it can easily be revitalized with rich, fiery colors, and although the room won't actually look any bigger it will certainly be more enticing. Depending on your personal decorating style, your room could be dark,

left Deep mahogany walls provide psychological support and protection in a cozy room.

below The rich colors and textures of the cushions and fake fur throw on this corner seating unit offer tactile and sensory pleasure in a cool, contemporary setting.

heavy, grand, and ornate, or have a light, bright, and friendly atmosphere. Either way, comfy seating and soft lighting should be used to create a sense of intimacy.

Playrooms also lend themselves to a red color scheme. Bright red is not only cheerful, it positively encourages physical movement and so is well suited to activity areas in the home. A den or workroom will come alive if decorated with a variety of stimulating colors. However, bright colors need not always be reserved for the walls but can be introduced into the furniture and furnishings instead. Inexpensive work tables, shelving, and seating can be given a new look with a coat of eggshell or gloss paint, while colorful cushions, rugs, and soft furnishings can also create a fun-filled space.

opposite The bold use of shiny red doors not only provides useful storage space in a small kitchen but also brings energy and vitality as you walk through to other rooms.

left Red accents on the drapes and cushions add a touch of the exotic and a sense of drama to a neutral room.

right At heart, this is a classic combination of red and white. The assuredness of these contrasts is underlined by the classic materials on offer: leather, glass, wood, stone, and terracotta.

color palette

passion **flower**

FOR OTHER SENSUAL OR
LUXURIOUS COLORS, SEE ALSO:

THE SPIRIT OF RED **42**

EMERALD RICH **172**

THE SPIRIT OF VIOLET **184**

DEEP PURPLE **188**

Through the ages, the color red has always been associated with love. Red is linked to the planet Venus and is a color that stimulates passion and touches our hearts. When surrounded by red, our heartbeat quickens, our pulse rate increases, and we become hot and excited, so it is not surprising that we can use this color to celebrate our sexuality. Deep shades of red stimulate the physical senses while softer pinks and lilacs play a more gentle and loving role, but all of these tones can be used to create an intimate and relaxing space.

An exotic-red bedroom does not have to be heavy and dark. Rich tones of purple, claret, and gold will create an air of luxury without making the space feel confined. Making the ceiling color light will keep the room from looking dark and dreary during the day. And if you use soft, flowing materials to drape a four-poster bed, or for a window treatment, the gentle breeze through the fabrics will prevent the room from looking heavy and becoming uncomfortably hot. Note that while a bed decorated in deep, rich red, purple, and pink could be your perfect den of passion, it could also be a difficult

place to sleep. The answer to this dilemma may lie in dressing your bed in the colors of love while keeping the decor of the rest of the room in more neutral and relaxing tones.

Contrasting textures are the key to stimulating your sense of touch and helping you connect with your physical body. To create your exotic boudoir, select soft linen and textured throws and cushions in silk, satin, or brocades. Try to find fabrics shot with gold

opposite A deep red wall is the main feature that brings warmth and sensuality to this simple bedroom.

below The bed has been dressed with hot pink cushions—and a vase of flowers added for that special occasion.

right The use of subtle
and contrasting shades
of pink-red and
gray accentuates the
grounded quality of
the bed in this
sophisticated Japanese-
style bedroom.

right An unusual combination of violet and pink-red creates an air of mystery and opulence.

thread, or bed covers with sparkling borders. Soft lighting and beaded lampshades will add extra sparkle.

If deep red and violet are really not to your liking, you can still bring romance to your bedroom by using lighter tints.

THINK PINK

Pink is the softer side of red and can range from deep, vivid shades to almost white. Like red, pink can be hot or cool in temperature. Hot pinks are vibrant and sexy, especially when teamed up with orange and red. These

bright pinks are a favorite with teenagers and their popularity came to the fore when pop art became fashionable in the 1960s. Cool pinks can be clear and bright and look fresh when combined with green and white, creating soft, feminine spaces that work well in a country-house setting.

Deep tones also contrast well with green, and rose or salmon pink look stylish and romantic when set against light blue. Other pinks are dusky and muted; they contain cool tones of gray and blue, which make them particularly versatile so that they coordinate

opposite A classic and romantic pink and white color scheme is the perfect way to keep a spare bedroom looking fresh and clean.

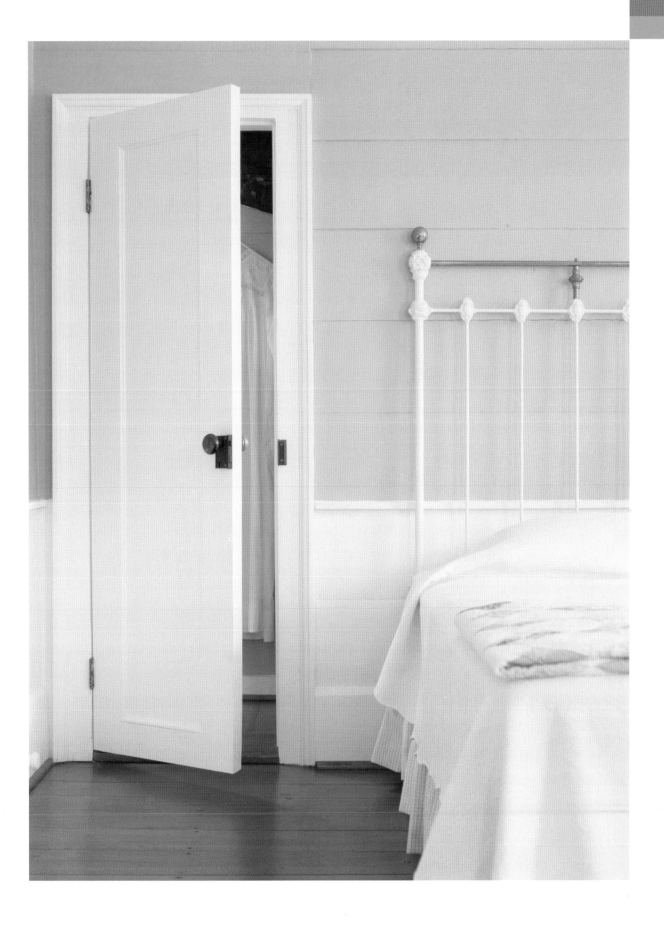

right The deep Etruscan red walls add a modern twist to a classic white bathroom and make an alluring and nurturing space adjoining the master bedroom.

well with other colors—such as red, yellow, blue, and even brown.

Deep rose-pink or pale cherry-blossom pink both have a warm tone that creates a gentler mood. These tones look good in a traditional bedroom. A Victorian-style brass bedstead or country-pine bed would fit in well too, especially with mixed-and-matched printed wallpapers and fabrics. Lilac and orchid are cool pinks that work well when set against dark wood and lend themselves to a more sophisticated style.

You can dress your bed with textured linens and covers in silky or satin finishes to make your boudoir even more enticing. If you are going for a modern style, use sheepskins and fake fur for rugs and cushions.

FOR OTHER EXCITING OR
ENERGETIC COLORS, SEE ALSO:

EXOTIC SPICE **104**

SHOCKING PINK **204**

SWEET PASTELS **224**

When you need fun and laughter in your life, think orange. This bright and cheerful color is eye-catching and brings a sense of friendliness and welcome. Its uplifting energy is a tonic if you are feeling health, happiness, and well-being. Orange makes a bold statement and is a favorite with outgoing personalities and the young at heart. It expresses freedom and optimism and so is popular at times of prosperity.

the spirit of **orange**

Bright and cheerful, warm and welcoming, orange is linked in our minds with health, fitness, and fun—all qualities that create a happy, sociable atmosphere.

color palette

depressed, and on a dull day, a splash of orange lifts the spirits. Our associations with vibrant orange are sensuous—to the eyes and the stomach. Who can resist a plump ripe peach or juicy orange? Who does not regard an orange sunset as a feast for the eyes? The comfort and feel-good factors that make orange so attractive may be the reasons why it is the color most associated with

Orange is the meeting point between red and yellow—not as hot or intense as the former, nor as bright and airy as the latter. Its in-between quality makes it ideal for linking other hues of similar or contrasting families.

HOW ORANGE AFFECTS A ROOM

Orange tones blend well with a gold and green scheme and enhance the natural qualities of wood without being too oppressive. Deep-orange hues make a room look smaller. Less hot than reds, a small room decorated in this color always appears cozy and inviting.

The color is often associated with fire, and this gives it a warming quality that draws us into an orange space. An entrance area decorated in shades of orange and brown

right Fire colors bring a feeling of warmth, movement, and change to a room.

left The deep blue glass lights add a calming influence in this bright and cheerful child's room.

use orange to

- make a bold, eye-catching statement

- draw people into a space

- give a warm welcome

- make a friendly, sociable space

- create a warm, cozy room

- evoke an earthy style

gives a hearty welcome. Psychologists have found that when exposed to orange, people tend to feel relaxed and emotionally secure and so talk to each other more. Thus its "sociable" qualities make it a good choice for spaces used for dining and entertaining.

ORANGE COLOR SCHEMES

The majority of people think of orange as a strong and intense color, but it has many guises. When mixed with yellow it becomes a rich apricot or tantalizing mango. If a little white is added, it transforms into a soft peach. Bright orange can be brash and loud—useful if you want to create a central focus. Softer shades are perfect in areas where you want to create a quieter atmosphere but still maintain natural warmth; use them to create a more sophisticated feeling in living areas or comfortable bedrooms.

As orange can be very intense and spicy, it is not usually considered a restful color and so is often used in interiors to convey a sense of movement, travel, and adventure. It is well suited to modern schemes, especially to reflect a dynamic, outgoing lifestyle. However,

below The orange units and tawny countertop emit an inviting glow that creates a sense of enclosure in a large, open-plan space.

left Being greeted by a large, comfortable chair gives an immediate sense of welcome and sociability to the room, especially when it is colored orange.

a whole room in orange can be overwhelming and so it is better used as an accent on one wall or to highlight an architectural feature.

We associate orange with fall, and when toned down it turns into a luxurious rich copper or takes on a deep amber hue—colors that nourish, calm, and soothe us. Burnt orange and burnt sienna are rich and appealing, lending themselves to homes decorated in a Mediterranean style. You can make the most of these earth tones by introducing terracotta tiles on the floor and earthenware ornaments around the room.

Oranges reflect little natural light, but with an open fire or good accent lighting can make a dark interior come alive. Earth tones add coolness without losing their hospitality, and so are well suited to homes in hot areas. Team orange with cool blues and greens for comfortable, relaxed living. Combine bright orange with more restrained tones to give wider appeal, while retaining the color's vitality.

FOR OTHER WARMING OR COZY
COLORS, SEE ALSO:

golden **glow**

Orange makes the perfect setting for dining, whether for a family meal or a quiet, romantic dinner for two. Not only has it been found to offer us psychological support, it also has a beneficial effect on our appetites, so that we can relax and enjoy our meal.

This instinct to eat in places where we feel relaxed and protected may have come from times when we ate around a campfire, where the golden glow of the flames afforded safety from attack. In an indoor dining room we can use golden orange decor to re-create this feeling of security, and even in an open-plan dining area, the glow from candles on a table will have a similar effect. Flame colors look good at night as they reproduce the magnetic quality of a fire, and during daylight, lend themselves to a relaxed, informal eating area.

opposite Natural light creates a bright, comfortable dining area by day; at night, the glow from the walls offers a more intimate and relaxed space.

right A few carefully chosen ornaments provide a simple way to bring warmth and vitality to a room.

color palette

color palette

right The orange tree is a clever way of enhancing the citrus and lavender blue theme, which is reminiscent of summer days.

Modern homes often have more than one eating area. A formal dining room is now mainly used for special occasions, while the family often prefers to eat informally in the kitchen or breakfast nook. As gold tones bring the naturalness of sunlight into a room, they are very flexible and suit all types of dining space. Light, creamy yellows are better for bright breakfast areas and conservatories, while deeper tones are more appealing in darker rooms that may be used in the evenings. Yellow is a happy and uplifting color for a kitchen–diner and it is likely that a large farmhouse kitchen decorated in this color will be a busy hub of home life.

All golden tones are excellent for enhancing the natural beauty of wood, and a flame-colored wall makes natural timber furniture take on a golden patina. We are much more likely to spend time in a space that uses these warm hues, and so it is not surprising that restaurants with a golden decor seem to offer a more intimate, friendly, and sociable atmosphere that really draws us in.

Warm tones need not be confined to indoor spaces; they look equally good when used for outside eating areas. Handmade terracotta tiles have a natural orange tone that brings a more intimate quality to outdoor entertainment areas and can be used to tile a patio, or cover weatherproof seats and tabletops. No outdoor eating area is complete without a barbecue or pizza oven, and an adobe-style oven can be made easily using face bricks. These can be left as they are, or rough-plastered in a traditional Spanish style and then painted in warm pink or orange for an authentic look.

below Light reflecting off the terracotta tiles enhances the beauty of the timber chairs and makes the room feel more enclosed.

right Good lighting
reflected off the pale
yellow walls is the key
to the success of this
multifunctional room.
The blue hanging lights
add a more intimate
ambience to the
dining space.

FOR OTHER WARMING OR COZY
COLORS, SEE ALSO:

RED COCOON **54**

GOLDEN GLOW **72**

GOLDEN CORN **112**

FALL HUES **218**

peaches and **cream**

There is something old-fashioned about peaches and cream, as these colors conjure up images of New England complexions and relaxed country living. Peach and cream is a special combination that can give a formal living room a graceful elegance or a cottage room a warm, country feel. Town houses also look good when decorated in these shades, as peach can lift a dark, urban environment.

Orange may be eye-catching and bright, but like all colors, it has a softer side too. The soft, blush tones of peach and apricot cannot fail to appeal as these gentle hues warm and nourish the body and soul. Peach is a tint that

right Color contrasts
can come from
surprising places and
the greenery outside is
the perfect complement
to the warm peach
tones inside.

left Changing the colors of the cushions and accessories is a good way of introducing seasonal moods into a living room.

color palette

is less dramatic than orange and when teamed with deep pink and cream it creates a timeless romantic style. So these light yet warm tones are suitable for all types of rooms, and if used as the basis of a color scheme for an entire house can create a feeling of space and continuity between rooms. An especially attractive effect can be achieved by varying the tone of peach and cream in different rooms, creating a subtle layered effect when looking down a passageway or through a door into a room.

On its own, pale peach and cream can look insipid unless some deeper accent colors are added. For a harmonious scheme, include rich apricot, pale gold, or terracotta, or for

right Combining harmonious colors and varying the tones used creates the feeling of spaciousness and flow through the rooms.

color palette

above The classic turquoise door sets off the warm and inviting hallway. As you enter, you really feel that you have come home.

more contrast, use green or blue. Blush shades always look better if contrasted with darker-toned wood. Mahogany, which has a reddish tinge, works best as the light reflected off a tabletop or floor will enhance the wall color.

Cream is particularly versatile, providing the perfect backdrop to other colors without

the harshness of white. Rich cream combines

well with blue to create a feeling of harmony

and serenity in a room. Peach also enhances

other colors, but a rich apricot or dusky pink

can also be at the heart of your color scheme.

Colors that will enhance these tones include

yellow, lilac, green, copper, and brown.

above The blue mosaics have prevented this yellow bathroom from becoming too sickly, and give a more relaxing atmosphere to the bathing area.

color palette

right Different flooring
textures and subtle
color contrasts help to
define the areas in this
multifunctional room.

FOR OTHER GROUNDING OR
EARTHY COLORS, SEE ALSO:

NEUTRAL SPIRIT **214**

WOOD AND STONE **220**

rustic **earth**

Since the dawn of time, people have built their homes from earth and so when we are surrounded by earth-colored objects and materials we feel comfortable and homely. Two natural earth tones are ocher and burnt sienna, and when blended together they create an orange that has a rich, tawny hue.

Earth colors are warm and embracing and make us feel rooted and connected. They look good anywhere in the home but if you don't want to decorate a whole room in earthy tones you can still introduce rich ocher or brown into the flooring and furniture. These deeper tones create a visual

right The hand-baked clay tiles and rustic furnishings help to bring a touch of the exotic indoors and make the house more homely.

color palette

left A rough stone and timber fireplace provides the central feature for the whole house and one that has a magnetic quality that draws you in to the building.

anchor and foster a strong connection with nature so we feel comfortable and secure.

Earth colors lend themselves especially well to a rustic country style, which can be as diverse as a log cabin in the woods or a Mexican hacienda in the desert. They give a lived-in feeling to a home, and chunky materials such as timber, baked clay tiles, and roughly plastered walls will accentuate the rustic look. The trick here is to combine them with lots of contrasting colors and not to make anything look too perfect. A room containing collections of books, pictures, and ornaments will feel more personal and inviting when you display them against a backdrop of earth colors.

Natural paints are made of earth pigments and are therefore excellent for creating a rustic atmosphere, making a room appear honest and authentic. These types of paints will weather and gently fade over time, giving a room a history. Broken color is a technique of overlaying color with a thin wash so that the base color shows through the top layer of glaze. In a rustic interior, this look gives the impression that the house has been painted by several occupants over the years, and also gives an interesting three-dimensional quality to heavy dark hues as the color changes when viewed under different lighting. Colorwashes using burnt sienna over yellow ocher will make a small space such as a staircase glow with light and energy, and a colorwash in an earth tone will instantly bring a neutral wall to life.

right This stylish basin and unit demonstrate that natural materials need not always be rustic but can be incorporated into a contemporary setting.

color palette

left Varying the intensity
of the tones from black
and brown through to
cream and white gives
a room an added
dimension and creates
more visual interest.

right Earth tones need not be hot and fiery, as shown in this cool, relaxing sitting room, where liveliness is created through the use of a geometric pattern.

color palette

FOR OTHER VIBRANT OR BOLD
COLORS, SEE ALSO:

ROYAL WELCOME **46**

SHARP CONTRASTS **222**

If you are a sun worshipper, you will love yellow. This is the color we perceive the sun to be and so we instinctively think of golden yellow as a powerful bringer of life and naturally find it positive and uplifting.

found all over the planet and, since ancient times, this color has been used as an artist's pigment. Ocher is much more muted than bright yellow and its earthiness helps create a feeling of comfort and stability. So the spirit of

the spirit of yellow

This color helps us to feel a tangible link with the place in which we live, yet it also appeals to the spiritual and more imaginative sides of our nature.

color palette

Yellow is the brightest of all colors and the most visible. When we look at yellow, therefore, our minds become stimulated, active, and alert. This makes it a very attractive color that can be used to create a vibrant, energetic atmosphere in the home.

The special qualities of yellow work on our psyche too. We hold yellow in high esteem, as it is the color of precious metal, thus golden hues speak of wealth and luxury. However, gold is also connected to spiritual wealth; our "golden years" bring us a feeling of contentment, and so yellow is often used to symbolize wisdom, illumination, and achievement.

Golden yellow is not only associated with the sun; the earth produces its own kind of yellow too. Yellow ocher is a natural earth

yellow is two-fold; on the one hand, it stimulates our intellect and on the other, it makes us feel grounded and connected with our home.

HOW YELLOW AFFECTS A ROOM

Yellow decor gives a room a warm, sunny appearance and will create the feeling of being in a light, bright space, even though this color doesn't actually make a room look larger. Rather than reflecting a great deal of light, yellow creates a glow of natural warmth that looks equally good in a large or small room.

Yellow is a warm color but without the heat of red or orange. Rather than stimulating the body, yellow energizes the mind, and when we are exposed to it, it can have a beneficial effect on our analytical capabilities

left This kitchen is filled with a golden glow, making it a cheerful and social place.

use yellow to

- make a warm, inviting space

- lift a dark, dreary room

- create a bright, cheerful atmosphere

- help wake you up in the morning

- make you more optimistic and positive

- highlight a space and make it more visible

and memories. The more we live our lives indoors away from nature and natural light, the more attractive yellow becomes. Use it in day rooms or areas where you spend a lot of time as it will keep you active and enable you to maintain a positive frame of mind.

As it is such a bright color, yellow has the capacity to reflect any other dominant color in the room, especially if the dominant color falls directly within the path of the light source. A yellow wall will therefore look green when placed next to a window overlooked by a tree or lawn, and blue carpet may take on a green hue from the reflected light from a yellow wall. To counteract the problem

of reflection you could soften the light by filtering it through white blinds or curtains, or change the tone of the carpet or furnishings to warm colors as these will be enhanced by the warm tones of the yellow.

opposite A combination of light drapes and yellow walls makes the most of the natural light and turns a landing into a place where you can linger.

WARNING SIGNS

Yellow is one of nature's warning colors. When placed next to black it becomes highly visible and so this combination of colors can be found on many stinging insects. Many road signs also make good use of this striking contrast.

There is no doubt that yellow is a powerful color and so should be used with care. Yellow has been found to stimulate the nervous system; for some people, exposure to too much yellow can make them feel irritable and uncomfortable. Some yellow tones have a green undertone and when viewed under electric lights can turn a sickly hue. It is therefore a good idea to test out yellow paint under both natural and artificial lighting conditions before you make your final selection.

mellow **yellow**

FOR OTHER RELAXING OR
SOOTHING COLORS, SEE ALSO:

THE SPIRIT OF BLUE **120**

DEEP INDIGO **142**

THE SPIRIT OF GREEN **152**

Yellow is not all sizzle, but can be laid back and mellow too. And if mixed with white, it takes on a rich, creamy tone that can prove invaluable to a home decor scheme. If you want a neutral look without the coldness of white, a soft yellow reflects light perfectly while still allowing you maximum flexibility in your choice of accent colors. The more yellow tends toward orange and the more muted the tone, the less likely it is to take on an acid hue at night. These mellow yellows create an informal, relaxed atmosphere in a room and look especially good when contrasted with deep blue or with lilac accents.

Rich, cream walls are extremely versatile and work well in both modern and traditional

right A color scheme based on creamy yellow and soft neutrals is relaxed, friendly, and easy to live with.

settings, and for monochromatic schemes in

living areas and bedrooms, especially when

set against the rich, deep tones of natural

materials such as timber or brick. Cream

always has a luxurious look and choosing

textured furnishings and fabrics can enhance

above Shiny black doors and Chinese yellow walls create an exotic bedroom that symbolizes both night and day, while the single orchid provides a point of focus when you enter.

color palette

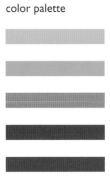

right During the day, creams and yellows give this dining room a relaxed and informal atmosphere. At night, the colors become more intense, making the space more supportive and intimate.

left The picture arrangement and yellow accents have created a sense of security and protection in this serene relaxation corner.

its beauty. A thick sheepskin rug adds a soft, lush feel to a bedroom floor, while a cream wool throw can enrich an outdated sofa. Remember, though, that cream can get dirty, so it is best to choose washable fabrics for drapes and upholstery. Go for a creamy tone if you want to keep the space light, or introduce a natural ocher for a richer look. Cream also

above A sense of playfulness and fun has been brought to this kitchen with the use of randomly placed blue and yellow tiles.

color palette

left By keeping the walls and ceiling the same tone of yellow, a sense of unity and space has been achieved. This contrasts with a color scheme that defines the different areas of the room (see pp. 84–85).

works well in passageways and hallways, as it brings a lighter appearance to areas that may be deprived of natural light.

Primrose yellow is a light color that is bright and cheerful in a kitchen or breakfast area and more suitable than egg yellow, which can be overpowering first thing in the morning. Light yellows can make a small bedroom or study more friendly and inviting, particularly if the room is in a dark area of the house. Keep the woodwork a glossy white to make sure the room looks clean and fresh.

Light yellow looks good when combined with blue as the two colors work in harmony, and you will also benefit from the relaxing qualities that blue has to offer.

right Lime green has both a bitterness and a shocking quality that can be used to grab your attention.

opposite An innovative breakfast bar features frosted glass to maximize the natural light flooding in and to enable you to enjoy the view outside.

exotic **spice**

color palette

When yellow turns to green it takes on a definite lemony zest. Lemon yellow can give you a wake-up call that is young and enthusiastic, and being much cooler than other yellows creates a bright yet clean atmosphere. It is best used in kitchens, morning rooms, and breakfast areas, as citrus colors are most attractive in natural light and can otherwise go a sickening acid yellow.

Lemon turns to lime when more green is added, and loses some of its brightness. Though lime is more soothing than lemon, it is still more lively and uplifting than pure green. Combine lime green with deeper citrus colors such as orange and gold for a harmonious scheme, or contrast it with deep blue for a more grown-up and relaxed style.

The youthfulness of citrus color schemes makes them popular with young people. The green quality brings a quieter influence to a child's bedroom while the brightness of the yellow ensures that it is a happy and fun space. However, if your child is hyperactive, a lime-colored room can prove a problem. In this case, it is important to contrast the lime green with blue, which will cancel out the mentally stimulating qualities of the yellow and enhance the calming qualities of blue.

right The fizzing pattern
on the room divider
is enhanced by
the pale lemon walls
and green chairs.

left The lime walls add a refreshing sizzle to the eclectic mix of materials and styles in this corner bathroom.

above The lime green walls ensure you'll wake up refreshed if you fall asleep in this comfortable old chair.

color palette

right Complementary tones of violet and yellow create balance in this bedroom, where the purple wall aids deep sleep and the yellow one provides a joyful wake-up call.

color palette

color palette

right Golden tones
reflect light well and
offer a feeling of natural
comfort and warmth.

opposite The cool
marble tiles and cream
and white color scheme
promise a calm retreat,
especially when viewed
through the bright
yellow door.

golden **corn**

In late summer and fall, the afternoon sunlight bathes everything in a golden glow and you cannot help but feel lazy and relaxed. This is the time when crops mature and nature's bounties are ready for harvest. Bringing these fresh golden tones indoors can give a warm glow to a dark or muted room, creating an easygoing, informal atmosphere.

These tones can also make a small space cozy and warm, while a larger space takes on a rich, earthy tone, inviting you to relax with family and friends. In winter, golden yellow

brings summer warmth inside. In summer, natural tones of golden brown are suitable for outdoor eating areas, especially if contrasted with cool turquoise or blue.

Near the pool or in the garden, an outdoor setting in blue contrasts well with the natural environment. Choose a blue-checked tablecloth or blue-striped cushions on dining chairs to remind you of a sunny vacation.

Golden corn reflects the richness of nature, but the association of yellow with the naturally occurring metal, gold, means that golden tones also look particularly good in metallic finishes. Gilded furniture, gilt picture frames, and shiny fabrics are opulent and luxurious, and if used sparingly can create a point of focus in any room.

The qualities of gold can be enjoyed very simply without using it directly as a wall color or in your decor at all. If you have a light-filtering blind or drape, your room will naturally be filled with a golden light, and you can enhance this effect by choosing pale yellow, cream, or ivory walls, as the sunlight will deepen the tones.

Like corn, sunflowers and lavender fields are powerful images often associated with

the beauty of the places in which they enjoy a hot, dry climate. Yellow and violet are complementary hues on the color wheel and can make for a dramatic and appealing color scheme. However, it is best to vary their tones; for example, a bright yellow combines better with a pale lavender, while a deep violet looks good with a light cream. Neutral schemes are popular in modern apartments. However, living in an all-neutral environment can take its toll psychologically. Harvest colors do not have to be bright, and gold is easily toned down if combined with light, natural tones that suit an urban environment.

Tan, beige, and cream harmonize well with gold, and darker tones of brown and gray-green will make a room calmer and more relaxing without leaving you feeling tired and bored.

opposite A mixture of mat and shiny surfaces creates an exciting interplay of finishes and colors in this farmhouse kitchen.

left The blue-violet color of the sea is complemented by the yellow tones of the chairs and sofa.

color palette

right The complementary tones of blue-gray and soft cream create a comfortable but relaxed living room, which is further enhanced by the natural patina of the timber floor and coffee table.

color palette

the
blue family

Since we live on a blue planet, the color blue takes on a special significance—it is closely associated with the life-giving forces of sky and water. The blue family is far-reaching and offers a range of hues from light, fresh turquoise through to deep indigo. Pastel blues are soft and gentle, while tones of green-blue are refreshing and cleansing. Deep blue affects our metabolism and body clocks and, like the midnight sky, has a sedating effect, slowing down all our body systems so that we instantly begin to feel calm, soothed, and relaxed.

FOR OTHER RELAXING OR
SOOTHING COLORS, SEE ALSO:

MELLOW YELLOW **96**

DEEP INDIGO **142**

THE SPIRIT OF GREEN **152**

Blue has a quiet, peaceful spirit, a thoughtful and dignified quality that is invaluable in a noisy, busy world. Information overload is fast becoming a problem that is affecting our mental and

blue personality is intuitive and knowledgeable and expresses itself in all forms of creative activity. Those who like blue are often introverted souls who prefer a quiet life. Alternatively they may be seeking a quiet

the spirit of **blue**

Calming, soothing, and healing, blue conveys an essence of the deeper realms of the spirit, and can bring inspiration and dream-like qualities to the home.

color palette

physical health; here, the special healing quality of blue creates physical space and also allows us plenty of room to think things over and put our lives into perspective.

Although essentially a cold color, blue is not unfriendly as it has many symbolic meanings that make it attractive to us. We associate blue with peace, and therefore many peacekeeping organizations around the world use it in their logos. In various cultures, blue is seen as providing a link with the heavens and the spirit, giving it an aura of protection. It is a color that gives out a message of trust, friendship, and loyalty.

Blue is a solitary color, preferring to relax and withdraw rather than party and socialize. However, it is certainly not tired and boring. A

haven if they need time to heal or if they lead a hectic lifestyle. The caring nature of blue makes it a popular color with doctors and teachers, and psychologists have found that we become more attracted to blue the older we get. Most people give blue as their favorite color. Its calming nature means we are particularly attracted to this color when

above right A blue sofa provides a place where you can relax and unwind in an atmosphere of quiet and sophistication.

left Wall panels have been turned into a work of art with a harmony of muted blue and gray paint that is both beautiful and soothing to the eye.

use blue to

- bring peace and calm

- cool down a hot or stuffy room

- increase the size of a small space

- make a room look fresh and clean

- help you sleep

- help combat a stressful lifestyle

we need to spend some quiet time on our own, and it can be used in the home to promote respect for one's personal space. Its quiet strength and fluidity helps us connect with our inner selves and brings out our best.

HOW BLUE AFFECTS YOUR ROOM

To make a room feel larger, decorate in pale blue. Generally, blue has the effect of making walls recede so that a room appears bigger, although this effect also depends on the tone you use. Light blue mimics the openness of the sky and makes a space appear light and airy. Dark blue reflects little light and so draws the room in.

Blue is at the cold end of the color spectrum and so can make a hot room appear cool. But too much dark blue can

below Stainless steel reflects the cool lavender tones to give a sleek and spacious feeling in a small kitchen.

make a space look unfriendly and depressing. In a room used during the day, the solution is to mix blue with light or bright warm colors to keep it vibrant and bright. In bedrooms and bathrooms, deep blue can be used for accents, creating a comfortable and relaxing space without seeming dark and cold.

When blue moves toward green it takes on a warmer hue. Turquoise has a depth and brilliance that is often associated with the tropical ocean, and for this reason can give a room real impact. Deep blue-green is highly saturated and vibrant, bringing vigor and warmth to a room. But in large areas it can become too dominant, and because it has a warm undertone, may influence other colors such as yellow, making them appear dirty or harsh. Red works well in direct contrast to bright turquoise, but it is important to make sure the red doesn't become too harsh and the room therefore too overpowering.

Blue is the color most often associated with night, so whatever tone of blue you use, it will bring stillness and serenity to a room. During the evening, little natural light enters our eyes and this naturally slows down our mental and bodily processes.

Similarly, the calming influence of blue in our surroundings can make us relaxed and sleepy. Decorating in blue is therefore perfect in areas of your home where you want to sit and rest. Remember, though, that the deeper the tone of blue, the more sedative it becomes, and so use it sparingly to accent other harmonious colors or as a contrast to bright, warm tones.

below Crisp white bed linen and pale aqua walls create a light, airy, and refreshing bedroom.

heavenly **blue**

FOR OTHER COOLING OR
REFRESHING COLORS, SEE ALSO:

AQUA SURF **132**

SPRING GREENS **156**

COOL MINTS **164**

LAVENDER FIELDS **196**

ALL WHITE, ALL RIGHT **226**

If you gaze into the blue heavens on a clear day, or into a cool blue ocean, you will feel calm and soothed. Blue is therefore a color we never seem to tire of, and we can happily live with large expanses of blue in our home and work environments. As most people like this color, it has always been popular in home decorating. However, while it may seem an easy option for a color scheme, a blue room can end up looking cold and uninviting unless the right combination of tones is used.

Blue is essentially a cool color and the more it tends toward the red or lilac end of the spectrum the cooler it becomes. Cool blues

color palette

right Contrasting blue with vibrant yellow and red creates balance and brings life and vitality to an otherwise cool room.

left The deep blue
bedding is reminiscent
of the ocean, inducing
relaxation, and aiding
in peaceful sleep.

above Relax in the bathtub and enjoy the therapeutic qualities of this simple white and duck-egg blue bathroom.

color palette

color palette

left Clean lines and pale, blue-gray units create a light and airy kitchen, while the bowl of apples adds a hint of color to this otherwise monochromatic color scheme.

have a quiet elegance and so lend themselves to a more formal setting. Rooms decorated in soft blues encourage quiet conversation rather than a party atmosphere.

Even though light blues reflect light, if pastel tones are used on their own they can make a room look too "sugary sweet." However, if light blue is mixed with darker tones, a room will look more sophisticated. Strong, deep blues work well in mat, eggshell, or gloss on doors and woodwork, or can be incorporated into furnishings and accessories. To create more contrast, use pale blue next to warm colors as its coolness makes the blue areas recede, adding dimension to a room.

Large expanses of blue are found in nature, therefore a room decorated solely in blue, or with blue carpeting, is easy to live with and gives a home a calm and relaxing atmosphere. In Georgian times, duck-egg blue was a particular favorite in English homes, and blue-gray was once often used in Scandinavian homes. Later, pale blue was to become a trademark of the Victorian homes in New England and the simple Shaker style that remains popular today. Many of these

right A venetian blind
helps to soften the light
coming into this relaxing
haven. The muted tones
of yellow and blue
add to the serenity
of the room.

color palette

styles mix pale blue with other light, muted colors to create a timeless style. Harmonious schemes can be created by combining blue with ivory, beige, or dove gray—accent colors that can be used according to your mood.

Blue-and-white schemes have also been popular in the many different styles throughout history and combine well with patterned fabrics and blue-and-white ceramics.

Coordinating your color scheme around a special item is a perfect way to create a harmonious and pleasing room. For example, you could go for the fresh country look or base your design around a traditional blue-and-white Chinese lamp or willow-pattern plate. This combination always looks light and fresh, as the white will bring light into a space even if you are using darker shades of blue, and is

color palette

right A black-and-white color scheme can be stark and cold, but the blue accents in this room create a timeless elegance that is more appealing.

ideal if you want your colors to remain stylishly simple and monochromatic.

As blue is so closely associated with water, blue and white are naturally favored colors for beach houses and lakeside residences. Simple blue-and-white stripes give a simple, cool look that complements a seaside location, and pale blues or a darker Oxford blue can be used for more contrast.

left A bright bowl of oranges adds an element of fun and surprise in a calm, blue setting.

FOR OTHER COOLING OR
REFRESHING COLORS, SEE ALSO:

HEAVENLY BLUE **124**

SPRING GREENS **156**

COOL MINTS **164**

LAVENDER FIELDS **196**

ALL WHITE, ALL RIGHT **226**

opposite A dreamy
atmosphere is easily
created with a sky
blue and white color
scheme and simply
styled furniture.

aqua **surf**

There is something very hypnotic and appealing about the ocean. Its endless movement and ever-changing moods are a source of inspiration to us. The deep blues and greens in the sea are especially beautiful and one can happily spend hours watching the light move across the water. Therefore, when transferred to our own homes this color scheme gives us an immediate lift.

Although the sea is sometimes still and calm and at other times powerful and frightening, for most of us it is the breaking waves and fresh sea air that really make us feel alive. Bringing the colors of the sea into your home can trigger your imagination as well as happy memories. Turquoise and white is an excellent combination that conjures up images of the hot sun and azure sea. These

color palette

right A band of
contrasting blue gives
a neutral kitchen
an instant lift and
helps to set off the
timber units.

fresh, clear colors are a perfect combination for any room but are especially suited to hot bathrooms and kitchens.

Turquoise is a mixture of blue and green. It can look deep and saturated or light and airy. Unlike pure blue, which creates a relaxing stillness, turquoise has movement so that its effect is more like a refreshing shower than a long soak in the bathtub. Aquamarine is much lighter than turquoise and has more sparkle; however, both hues work well when harmonized with deep tones of blue and green. Oranges, crimsons, and golds can be added to give warmth, and turquoise or aqua can really shine when placed next to these sunset colors.

right Contrasting rich, tan cream with blue adds warmth to a cool bathroom. The reflected light enhances skin tones.

opposite The thin black tile border adds a classic touch to a simple blue and white bathroom.

right Frosted glass
doors create a
shimmering cloudscape
in this unusual
open-plan bedroom
and bathroom.

right A blue wall in a kitchen sets off both rustic garlic strings and contemporary kitchen utensils.

opposite The creative use of a vibrant blue countertop provides a dramatic and eye-catching feature in this cool kitchen.

The freshness and vitality of turquoise gives it an invigorating, contemporary quality that will bring lightness to most rooms. Deep turquoise tiles or pale aqua walls will look cool and stylish, while a living or dining area decorated in these tones will have a relaxed and informal feeling.

Electric blue is a clean, bright hue that lies between blue and turquoise. It has a refreshingly warm tone and a jewel-like quality that is much more vibrant and stimulating than most blues tend to be.

This color lends itself particularly well to a contemporary kitchen where it can be used for kitchen units, work surfaces, or tiling, and where it contrasts well with white and harmonizes with aluminum finishes and stainless steel equipment.

left A play of reflected
light produces less glare
when using muted tones
and modern materials
for countertops
and splashbacks.

FOR OTHER RELAXING OR
SOOTHING COLORS, SEE ALSO:

MELLOW YELLOW **96**

THE SPIRIT OF BLUE **120**

THE SPIRIT OF GREEN **152**

deep **indigo**

color palette

Blue is not always about simplicity. Deep rich blues are reminiscent of many palatial buildings around the world. These colors have often been used in cool courtyards and relaxation areas away from the heat of the midday sun. Indigo is especially relaxing. When spending time in a dark blue room it is easy to fall into a state of daydreaming or deep contemplation. While indigo on its own can make a whole room too cold and depressing, it can create a perfect quiet retreat in a nook or corner of a living room.

Deep blue need not be too melancholic. Rich blues are regal and stately, while other blues are more exotic and are suitable for an ethnic-style room. Deep ultramarine is particularly intense. It is made by grinding down the semiprecious stone lapis lazuli, a rare natural pigment that has a fine color and is very stable. Ultramarine reflects little light but creates a sense of mystery and opulence. It should be used sparingly in smaller rooms so that it does not lose its appeal. In larger spaces, it may be better to decorate

right The comfortable chairs with deep blue upholstery enhance a thoughtful environment for a game of chess.

left Indigo accents
provide points of focus
and accentuate the
sophisticated formality
of this living room.

right The dark-colored stairwell creates a sense of mystery as it leads the eye up to the light and relaxed mezzanine area.

opposite The indigo
bedcover adds
a sense of opulence
and luxury to a
minimalist bedroom.

with ultramarine or turquoise accented with rich earth colors such as burnt sienna or ocher, tones that bring a deep warmth and sense of luxury to an otherwise cold room. Clean white contrasts well with deep blue and is ideal for a nautical theme.

Indigo is a popular deep blue, and most people are familiar with indigo-dyed blue jeans. Indigo dye was originally obtained from plants and considered rather special for its color-fastness, becoming a luxury around the world as the chosen color for the attire of the rich and powerful. Similar to indigo is woad, another deep-blue dye, loved by ancient Britons, and rediscovered in 1880. Woad and indigo are still used to dye cloth, although increasingly replaced by artificial colors.

Being so dark, indigo blue is very cool and relaxing, but as it reflects little natural light its use is best restricted to fabrics and furnishings. Indigo is also eye-catching, and an indigo-dyed artifact makes a central point of focus in a living room. The best indigo pieces are found in antique tribal rugs and woven cloth. You can still find many beautiful and inexpensive fabrics combining indigo with white or madder red. Traditional designs from around the world include the tie-dye techniques popular in India, batik from Java, and Indonesian ikat designs.

right Shapes and colors at low level become more important when you are seated, and so this fireplace has been given added character by the positioning of the unusual cactus.

above The indigo day
bed makes a strong
statement in a
monochromatic color
scheme and adds
a welcome touch of
luxury in a cool,
contemporary setting.

the
green family

Nature and the color green are so closely connected that it is impossible to think of one without thinking of the other. Whether the pale green of new shoots in spring, rich grass green, or the deep blue-green of pine needles, green has special healing qualities. We instinctively seek out a green park or the countryside when we are feeling stressed so that we can refresh mind and body. It is the green pigment, chlorophyll, in the leaves that allows plants to harness the energy of the sun, and release the oxygen that creates a healthy atmosphere where all life can flourish.

FOR OTHER RELAXING OR
SOOTHING COLORS, SEE ALSO:

MELLOW YELLOW **96**

THE SPIRIT OF BLUE **120**

DEEP INDIGO **142**

Green is an easygoing color. Its close connection with nature helps to link us to the cycle of life so that we can relax and go with the flow. However, although green is quiet and calm, it is rarely still. Just as the many health benefits; it fortifies and restores the body, building up our immune systems and soothing our minds so that we can resist stress. Decorating a room in green creates a relaxing space where we can stop and breathe. In the

the spirit of green

The calming nature of green has made it a popular choice for decorating, and most homes will benefit from the harmonious atmosphere it creates.

color palette

spring brings hope and expectation of the summer to follow, green refreshes and cleanses our hearts and minds so that we can move on with renewed energy.

Green never looks out of place—for its position at the center of the rainbow means it is in harmony with all of the other colors. Green has

theater, the "green room" in which actors rest before a performance is designed to convey this calming quality. However, green can make you lazy and uninterested in life, so too much of this color is not a good idea for the indecisive or those who lack motivation.

When green turns to turquoise it takes on a more lively and invigorating personality, and is associated with the sparkling ocean that flanks unspoiled beaches in exotic locations.

HOW GREEN AFFECTS A ROOM

Indoors, green can be an elusive color—for its look and mood are constantly changing. If a room is filled with natural light, green can be cool and relaxing, but in a dark room it can absorb the light, leaving the space cold and

right Plants bring life and movement and a natural element into a room.

opposite Simple shapes and soft green colorings enhance this quiet, reflective corner.

use green to

- create a sense of calm

- cool down a hot, stuffy room

- provide time and space to breathe

- create a relaxed and stress-free atmosphere

- instill harmony and balance within the home

- create a refreshing haven

right The green family
of colors harmonizes
well with yellow
and their combined
use has made this
bedroom warmer and
more inviting.

color palette

uninviting. Lighter tints are useful on walls for a cool, relaxing haven, but because they reflect light well they make other colors appear more dominating than they actually are. Green always looks better in a mat or eggshell finish, as gloss paint tends to look institutional and muddy. Shiny green is best suited to exterior features where it can catch the light. Green doors, windows, and ironwork give a home a quiet, classical elegance.

Mid-green works best when combined with other colors and incorporated into upholstery and furnishings. Dark green can be foreboding, giving the feeling of being in a deep forest. However, cream and yellow can soon give it a lift and create a fresh, country style. Green color schemes are not usually associated with urban living, though cool, mint-green and aquamarine can bring a lightness into a modern setting.

If you decide to use green on walls, be careful as some greens turn sickly or muddy under artificial light. Cleaner tints are particularly versatile, creating a sense of peace and tranquillity, and are useful for creating a "layered" look using techniques such as dragging, stenciling, and colorwashing.

left Dark green walls create a sense of enclosure and accentuate the light-colored sofa and pictures.

left A fresh and light mood is created when the tones are similar, making the room feel bright and airy.

decorating with plants

Plants are the most natural way of bringing a green connection into your home. Not only are they alive and beautiful but they have important health benefits too. Scientists at the NASA space agency have conducted numerous experiments on the affects of indoor plants on the home environment. For example, they have found that plants not only clean the air but also absorb noise and electronic "smog," acting like natural ionizers; they are therefore useful in areas where electrical equipment is in use. Plants also absorb toxins such as formaldehyde and benzene that are given off by furniture, carpets, paints, and detergents. Ferns, ficus trees, philodendrons, and palms are all particularly good choices for homes or offices.

Plants also provide a simple and highly portable design feature. By moving plants around, you are moving color around your home. In a city apartment, plants contribute to architectural form, as well as creating a sense of peace and quiet in a bustling environment.

FOR OTHER COOLING OR
REFRESHING COLORS, SEE ALSO:

HEAVENLY BLUE **124**

AQUA SURF **132**

COOL MINTS **164**

LAVENDER FIELDS **196**

ALL WHITE, ALL RIGHT **226**

spring **greens**

As in nature, green makes an ideal backdrop for other hues, setting them off to perfection. This is especially true of dark green, which, like a verdant landscape, highlights and contrasts with most other colors.

So, the key to using green in your home is to mix it with other colors, because on its own it can become lifeless and dull. Green falls in the middle of the visible light spectrum. Its wavelength is neither long (like red) nor short (like blue). Similarly, its temperature is neither hot nor cold. Green holds a balance between all things and this adaptable quality means it can be successfully combined with either hot or cool tones.

The combination of green, gold, and yellow creates a young and fresh feeling. Combined with blue and violet it becomes luxurious and exotic, and when contrasted with red or orange produces a color scheme that scintillates. If using green for a mono-chromatic scheme, it is essential to vary the

opposite Green walls are less distracting and therefore enhance appreciation for these delicate ceramics and the details in the pictures.

color palette

right Silk cushions and the harmonizing border on these drapes bring to life a neutral scheme while retaining its restful qualities.

temperature and tones from light to dark to maintain movement and visual stimulation and prevent the room from becoming too cold and impersonal.

Spring green can bring a tired, dark kitchen back to life. In interior design, green is often thought of as a dull, old-fashioned color, but the right green can be sparkling and fresh. Imagine the top of a new shoot or celery stalk; pale yellow-green tints such as these are cool and light, and make a hot, stuffy room seem clean, light, and airy, a place where you will feel cool and refreshed. On its own, spring green can look cold and clinical, so it is best contrasted with deeper tones such as yellows, oranges, and browns.

As it is so strongly associated with nature, combining green with these natural tones ensures that a color scheme will look harmonious and balanced. If you are refurbishing your kitchen, a terracotta floor or timber units would give the kitchen natural depth and warmth, or you could include these colors in blinds or work surfaces.

color palette

Spring green gives a decorating scheme a spirit of evolution, so that it appears to change at different times of the day, month, or year, and with your moods. If combined with other natural tones, it will convey the feeling of natural abundance in the home.

Green brings a fresh, relaxing quality to a living room and so is easy to live with. As it goes with everything, green can be used without the worry that it will clash with other colors in a room. For example, these natural, harmonizing qualities work extremely

well in furnishing patterns, especially if the

~~designs incorporate natural forms, such as~~

plants and flowers. In fact, fabrics that incor-

porate green can be mixed and matched

much more easily than other hues, as this

color gives continuity to a decor.

color palette

above Alternate areas of light and shade and the rough and smooth textures of the drapes and upholstery combine to make a calm and elegant room.

color palette

right This Japanese design recognizes the contemplative qualities of the color green, and incorporates large sliding screens that maximize the view of the garden.

FOR OTHER COOLING OR
REFRESHING COLORS, SEE ALSO:

HEAVENLY BLUE **124**

AQUA SURF **132**

SPRING GREENS **156**

LAVENDER FIELDS **196**

ALL WHITE, ALL RIGHT **226**

color palette

cool **mints**

Mint green is one of the most refreshing colors you can use in interior design. As its name suggests, this pale green is cool and clean and acts in a similar way to the herbal mints used over centuries for medicinal purposes and for their refreshing aromas. Whereas leaf green and lime green have a warm tone, mint green is much lighter and cooler, with a sharper and more piercing quality.

Mint green comes into its own in spaces where you want to create a relaxed, light, and airy atmosphere. However, be careful that it doesn't become too stark and cold.

Cool mints work especially well in hot areas such as the kitchen, or anywhere you need to maximize space. If teamed up with neutrals, they can create a timeless elegance in a room. It is best to add a touch of brightness to a cool green room; purple, claret, or orchid furnishings inject some energy, but stay away from sugary pinks, which can make a room look like a candy store.

opposite Harmonies of rich cobalt blue and pale green bring visual interest—and a touch of the exotic—into this contemporary kitchen.

right Breaking up the large areas of green with white grout and varying the tones of the tiles prevents this bathroom from looking small and claustrophobic.

left Shiny, glazed
crockery in citrus colors
is a great conversation
piece and makes
the food look
more appetizing.

above Warm green
drapes prevent the large,
dark sofa from becoming
too dominant and help
separate the relaxation
and work areas.

In a large or open-plan area, mint takes on a cool, modern style. It can be used on walls, or in ceramic tiles and frosted glass. Large, tinted glass windows, screens, or even stairs in this color can make a dull room look special, while cool, mint-colored tiles can transform a claustrophobic bathroom or messy kitchen into a bright, crisp, inviting space. For a more vibrant color scheme, add extra blue to a light green to yield a stronger blue-green that works well on walls or woodwork. Alternatively, you can juxtapose green with other bright primary or secondary colors to give a room a more lively appearance.

opposite Being surrounded by natural objects and greenery makes bathing a more special and therapeutic experience.

left Contrasting tiles give this white kitchen a lift and a feel-good factor reminiscent of mellow white wine and flavorsome olive oil.

right Large panels of natural stone with a subtle green tinge set off this shiny white bathtub and lend weight to the open-plan room.

color palette

FOR OTHER SENSUAL OR
LUXURIOUS COLORS, SEE ALSO:

THE SPIRIT OF RED **42**

PASSION FLOWER **60**

THE SPIRIT OF VIOLET **184**

DEEP PURPLE **188**

emerald rich

color palette

Emerald green is the most dramatic of all the greens. It is made from a mixture of yellow and deep blue, and the more blue that is added, the richer it becomes. Emerald green pigment has a special luminosity that reflects its jewel-like origins. This special quality lends itself to the decoration of historical homes and classical architecture.

The oldest type of emerald green pigment was made from malachite, a precious stone held sacred by the ancient Egyptians and also the Chinese. Emerald green was first produced artificially in 1814.

right Taking inspiration from the combination of hues seen in nature is a foolproof way of using coordinated colors in home decor.

Today this is known as chrome green and is a mixture of blue and yellow pigments. It lends itself well to rooms used in the evening.

Dark greens give a feeling of security and protection, much like a forest glade, and you can make use of this quality in areas where you want to create a feeling of strength and privacy. Emerald green walls in a room look best if they have a shiny finish so that they are not too dark and dull.

A formal dining room decorated in an eggshell finish or glazed colorwash provides a wonderful setting for a banquet, while a hallway decorated in this color will show off classical paintings and historic photographs. Contrast green walls with warm-colored furnishings and table decorations to make guests feel cozy and comfortable.

Emerald green is perhaps the showiest of the greens, as it has a special luster when reflected by shiny surfaces. But the depth of tone of emerald green reflects little natural light itself, so rooms decorated in this color have an unworldly glow and air of mystery—a good choice for a bedroom. On its own, emerald green is too dark, but combined with

left Varying the tones of brown, green, and neutrals adds interest to this room and gives it depth and visual interest.

other jewel-like tones such as deep blue, rich pink, and magenta it creates a sensual and luxurious room. The family of harmonizing blues and greens contrasted with rich copper rivals the beauty of any gemstone, and conveys the depths of the ocean.

One of the most alluring places you will find emerald green is in the tail feathers of a peacock. Feathers not only glisten and refract light, they move and are soft to the touch, making them an inspirational design object.

A bedroom decorated using a peacock's feather theme will be exotic and enticing. The deep colors are not only restful but positively narcotic, spiriting you away to a place of your

opposite A frosted glass sliding screen gives a softer light and a more relaxing ambience to a bedroom.

below Light-reflecting surfaces and neutral tones help to make this room look more airy and spacious.

left Green Roman blinds and velvet cushions introduce a natural touch to a city bedroom that helps induce sleep and yet provides a refreshing atmosphere to wake up to.

above On their own,
gray or dark-green
kitchen units can look
tired and lackluster,
but a warm, vibrant
color can quickly change
the atmosphere and
inspire the cook.

color palette

dreams. Use shiny fabrics like silks and shantung for bed covers and cushions as these shimmer much like feathers. Hang tiny beads on to lamps to move and catch the light. You could base the style of an exotic bedroom on a historic theme, such as the 1920s, when peacock feathers were very popular, or combine these colors with an opulent oriental style. A neutral, modern bedroom would also benefit from the touch of richness and mystery that emerald green can provide.

left If the ceilings are high, as here, a deep green wall helps ground the room and creates a sense of protection for this relaxing space.

right The interplay of vertical and horizontal lines creates internal drama and acts as a frame for the stunning view out of the sliding doors.

the
violet family

The violet color family is exotic and luxurious, stimulating our senses as well as our minds. But while violet appears deep and intense, it is also the most abstract of all the rainbow hues. It is created by mixing red and blue, which yields a variety of highly saturated tones that reflect little light, look deep and mysterious, dark and foreboding, and often appear almost black. By contrast, lighter tints of lavender and mauve are gentle and uplifting, as these contain the nurturing qualities of blue and pink, and so offer emotional support and feed our souls.

FOR OTHER SENSUAL OR
LUXURIOUS COLORS, SEE ALSO:

THE SPIRIT OF RED **42**

PASSION FLOWER **60**

EMERALD RICH **172**

DEEP PURPLE **188**

Violet has a personality of depth and power. It is a color that lies at the very edge of the visible spectrum, and in the form of ultraviolet light, reaches out into other dimensions. Its rarity in nature gives it a pigments are quite rare. Purple dye or paint is difficult and expensive to make and has always been a color linked with power and luxury. It is still associated with royalty today. The special qualities of violet have led to it

the spirit of **violet**

The colors of the violet family bring a sense of luxury and elegance to a home, and when used sparingly, can add an element of mystery and surprise.

color palette

special aura, and when we look at something purple it has a depth and changeability that seems almost otherworldly.

Violet has long been a favorite with artists, writers, and musicians who often choose to surround themselves with this color when they work. The profundity of violet on the human psyche means that when it is introduced to our surroundings it can help unlock the doors to our inner visions and creativity. Lighter tints of violet are less intense and the gentle tones of mauve, lavender, and lilac can bring out the more intuitive side to our nature.

Our fascination with violet reaches back into the mists of time. Although purple is all around us, natural violet and purple

being the color with the most religious associations, its intensity filling most of us with awe and wonder. Indeed, the violet family is held in such high regard that it has come to represent the human qualities of dignity, modesty, and spiritual strength.

Deep blue-violet and violets that contain less red emphasize the power and mystery of the night and are often associated with magic, which may explain why these colors were popular during the psychedelic era of the 1960s. The supernatural power of deep violet can literally stop us in our tracks. Medical scientists now claim that this color has a sedating and even euphoric effect on our systems. This color can therefore enhance our lifestyles by helping us to enjoy deep,

left A special sofa can provide the starting point of a decorative scheme. Here, complementary colors of purple and yellow create a feeling of opulence.

use violet to

■ add a sense of drama and mystery

■ bring luxury and richness

■ promote deep sleep

■ give an element of surprise

■ unlock your creative powers

■ harmonize your mind and body

restful sleep, and in a frenetic world can help us take time out to just sit and daydream.

HOW VIOLET AFFECTS A ROOM

Violet is a heavily saturated color that acts in a similar way to the night sky by seemingly drawing us in. Its propensity to absorb so much light means it is a difficult wall color to use successfully in the northern hemisphere, as a room decorated in purple can soon become dark and oppressive. On the other hand, this darkness can become an asset if violet hues are used in a room where you want deep relaxation or to create a restful and luxurious atmosphere.

Purple always creates a strong contrast, so it is best used as an accent to enhance other colors and add depth to a room. The theatrical setting it creates is most effective when used in rich furnishings and fabrics. Violet will also make a dramatic statement on a wall you want to draw attention to, or in a hallway to make you stop and to hold your gaze when you arrive home.

opposite Highlights of color on this contemporary lamp create points of contrast to the stylish yet fun interior.

below Violet is not as hard as black and so makes this contemporary kitchen feel more stylish and welcoming.

deep **purple**

When decorating with purple, you need to think creatively. Try to find a different way of presenting this color that is unusual and surprising. It is not necessary to decorate a whole room in purple, as just one simple glass vase can make a strong visual impact. Alternatively, use purple on architectural features around your home or place a purple object in any unusual nooks or recesses. A metal staircase can look stunning when set against a purple wall, and muted gray-colored pillars or built-in bookcases also make the room memorable.

One of the best ways to introduce purple into a home is in the soft furnishings, drapes, and carpets. The oldest and most beautiful purple pigment was made from shellfish found around the Mediterranean Sea. Tyrian purple was a dye so treasured and expensive to produce that it was used by the Romans for the togas of their emperors and other high-ranking persons. Cochineal is another purple dye, made from the dried bodies of female insects that live on cactus plants in Mexico and Central America. If chemical processes are used, cochineal also produces a

right A deep purple chair adds an air of luxurious elegance to a neutral room.

red-purple color, but unlike Tyrian purple, it fades in sunlight. It was not until the mid-nineteenth century, with the discovery of analine, that it became possible to manufacture a really stable purple dye.

Using a purple color scheme will undoubtedly add a rich, luxurious feel to a home, and even a humble abode can rise to the occasion. For example, a faded sofa or plain bedcover suddenly takes on a new appearance with the addition of a selection of purple cushions, and purple-colored accessories and objects can also add a sense of surprise, making even the simplest room a special place. The colors of the purple family blend well together so there is no limit to the

color palette

left Deep purple
is the perfect foil
to set off a display
of photographs and
prints and chic
white furniture.

number of patterns and textures that can be combined. Adding to your collection can be fun too.

Purple and yellow are complementary colors. When used together, they will create a dramatic statement that is rich and opulent. If this combination is used for wall colors, tones will need to be chosen carefully and the intensity of these hues balanced with white woodwork and other light neutrals. In general, it is best to use yellow rather than purple for the walls, as it is bright and welcoming, and

below Golden light pouring through these drapes prevents the dark, muted colors from looking drab and uninteresting.

color palette

left Using purple accessories is a quick way to give personality and add impact to a neutral color scheme.

to use purple drapes, upholstery, and accessories to add drama and mystery. Vary the tones of purple from light to dark and include some reds and pinks to give the room a more lived-in look and to prevent it from resembling an opera stage set. One wall painted purple can make a central point of focus in a large room, especially if you hang a gilt-framed mirror to reflect more light.

Modern homes sometimes lend themselves to being decorated with several colors—the walls can even become a work of

color palette

above In this kitchen, the bold wall color makes a strong statement on the end wall and also highlights the rich timber units and granite worktop.

right A muted pale gray with a hint of purple gives this Oriental-style bedroom a sense of mystery and opulence.

art. Sandy yellow and dusky mauve enhance each other without having a tug-of-war for attention. Two strong colors can be overpowering but can be softened with the addition of softer pinks and lilacs. For contrast, green can prove a good choice and plants always look good against purple hues.

Its similarity to the night sky can make dark purple an unusual choice for a passageway or landing, especially if you want to display a collection of artwork, but good spotlighting is essential. In addition, a brass or gilded candelabra in the hallway or stairwell can really create a "wow" factor.

A COLOR FOR ALL SEASONS

You don't have to live with purple all of the time, as this is a perfect color to bring into your home for special occasions. In fall and winter, a table dressed in red and purple makes a perfect setting for a festive meal, particularly when teamed with gold candles and shiny napkins. But purple looks equally good in summer, and a window seat or relaxation area decorated in these colors will take on an exotic air reminiscent of faraway places in Asia and the Middle East.

color palette

FOR OTHER COOLING OR
REFRESHING COLORS, SEE ALSO:

HEAVENLY BLUE **124**

AQUA SURF **132**

SPRING GREENS **156**

COOL MINTS **164**

ALL WHITE, ALL RIGHT **226**

right The simplicity of these bold complementaries and eye-catching accessories creates a relaxing but inviting bedroom.

lavender **fields**

color palette

Artists throughout the centuries have been captivated by fields of lavender, and most of us find this attractive color holds the gaze. Like the aroma of lavender flowers, this is a color that has a sharp, piercing quality, leaving us feeling cool and refreshed. Lavender oil is renowned for its rejuvenating effect on our systems, and using this relaxing color in the home creates a special atmosphere that allows you time to replenish your energy and renew your enthusiasm for life.

When we think of lavender fields, we usually visualize warm, sunny days, and so lavender has a natural connection with warm, earth tones. For a vibrant scheme, contrast lavender with golden yellow or ocher. A cool or dark room benefits from yellow walls and lavender accents. For a warm room, combine cool and fresh lavender walls with yellow furnishings for a friendly and inviting atmosphere. Lighter tints of lavender are soothing and refreshing, and all the more so when combined with white.

The doors and windows of traditional whitewashed buildings in many Mediterranean countries are often painted with

opposite Highlighting architectural lines with a deeper color tone draws the eye and creates an interesting and harmonious color scheme.

right The pale lilac walls and ceiling create a feeling of elegance and spaciousness in this contemporary sitting room, while the sumptuous furniture allows you to feel pampered and relaxed. This contrasts with a more classic color scheme (see pp. 58–59).

lavender blue, and this classic scheme still works well in almost any home. White woodwork or white-painted furniture makes a perfect foil for both yellow and lavender and can give a relaxed country feel to a home. But lavender blue need not be confined to wall colors and fabrics. In France and Greece it is a popular choice for woodwork and painted country-style furniture, and a simple chair can be given a new lease on life if freshened up with lavender-colored paint with an eggshell finish.

Lavender is a pale violet, so it can be effectively combined with colors adjacent to purple on the color wheel. Lavender, blue, and green is a calm and soothing combination that can be used very successfully in furnishings in a living room or bedroom.

If combined with warm colors such as red and orange, lavender takes on a vibrancy that creates a particularly stimulating environment. These bright tones look good when used as accents against a neutral background. Try them as cushions on a tan leather sofa or upholster chairs in these shades to fill a room with energy and add a modern zest.

Lavender tones can be sophisticated too, especially if combined with neutrals such as

left Lilac walls set off this unusual bathtub and the clean lines of the blinds and storage trolley. Purple towels add a luxurious touch.

below Pale lavender touches give the room an air of cool serenity without detracting from the subtlety of the wall covering.

tan, beige, and chocolate. Dusky tones are effective when used as a broken color technique, as they provide a perfect backdrop to brightly colored furnishings and accessories. Mauve is a warmer shade of lavender that has a much more pink tone.

below Lavender and blue lie adjacent to each other on the color wheel and so always work well together, as can be seen here.

right The relaxing and frivolous qualities of lilac have been utilized to enhance the dreamy effect created by the net canopy in this bedroom.

shocking **pink**

FOR OTHER EXCITING OR
ENERGETIC COLORS, SEE ALSO:

THE SPIRIT OF ORANGE **68**

EXOTIC SPICE **104**

SWEET PASTELS **224**

opposite Energy and a sense of drama have been created by introducing pink and purple into this bathroom, which also displays a sense of enclosure and privacy.

below The unusual combination of orange and hot pink have turned this otherwise ordinary bedroom into a vibrant and sensual haven.

It seems that when it comes to decorating, pink is one color that we either love or hate. The problem lies in the fact that most of us think of pink as a light, sugary color more suited to a child's room than to the main living areas. But this view is not really accurate. Pink belongs to the same family as red and so has many of the qualities of that vibrant and sexy color. Therefore pink is not always soft and gentle. For example, raspberry, deep orchid, and fuchsia are all pinks and yet are striking and grown-up. The intensity and brightness of these pinks has led to them being described as "shocking pinks." Shocking pink isn't a modern invention. For centuries, shades of this color have been popular in the decorating schemes of many cultures around the world. For example, in India, bright pink is often used alongside other members of the red family and also linked to violet and blue. In South America, shocking pink can be found contrasted with turquoise. In China and Japan, rich pink is often set against black or deep blue.

The youthfulness and energy of shocking pinks make them suitable for areas of a home

color palette

color palette

left The cool lilac theme in this bedroom has been made more welcoming with the use of colorwashing, two-toned walls, and the addition of pink.

above Varying the tones from light to dark and using an unusual palette of sugar pink, blue, and plum creates a vivid effect that enhances this retrostyled room.

where you want to make a bold statement. In a modern kitchen or living area, bright pink can look good in furniture and finishes. Vinyl, linoleum, tiles, and plastics are all available in many shades of this color. In the bedroom, shocking pink works well for bed drapes, bedcovers, and linen as well as blinds and other soft furnishings. For a decadent and exotic look, you can also introduce pinks into

beaded curtains, frosted glass, candles, and table ornaments.

If pink isn't your favorite color, you may find that it has more appeal when used as an accent. Neutral tones of beige, gray, or tan can all be enhanced with rich pinks. Even just one pink chair or pink cushions on a chocolate leather sofa will transform a quite ordinary room into something special.

right The accessories in this living room are a combination of several different color families that work together to create a decadent and opulent look.

left This glistening kitchen has been given added personality and vitality by accenting walls in cobalt blue and hot pink.

color palette

the
neutral family

If you want to create an aura of peace and
uncluttered calm, think neutral. With frenetically busy
working lives, more and more people need a light,
airy space where they can relax away from the
stresses of the world. By choosing a neutral scheme,
you can bring a sense of serenity to any room, and if
used throughout the whole house, neutrals promote
circulation and increase the feeling of space. Neutral
hues can provide a passive background that sets off
other colors, or can be used on their own to create
a subtle scheme.

FOR OTHER GROUNDING OR
EARTHY COLORS, SEE ALSO:

■ RUSTIC EARTH **86**

■ WOOD AND STONE **220**

Neutrals may not be the most dramatic of colors but neither do they have to be dull and boring. In fact, a neutral color scheme can have as much variety of tone as any other color scheme. The many hues of the

spaces as quiet colors do not elicit the strong reactions we often have when faced with bright color schemes.

Many people avoid neutrals because they associate them with minimalist interiors.

neutral spirit

Neutrals are versatile, elegant, easy to live with, and can be adjusted to suit all types of property, including period-, rustic-, and modern-style homes.

opposite The interesting textures of wicker and natural fabrics create an interplay of geometric shapes that complement this calm and spacious room.

color palette

neutral family range from pale buff and stone to deep shades of chocolate and blue-black. When combined, these light and dark tones work together in an interplay of shadow and light that is both subtle and beautiful.

Many natural colors are commonly thought of as neutrals. These include varieties of gray, soft earth tones, gray-green, and misty blue. Neutrals never go out of fashion, and a home decorated in these muted shades will have an air of sophistication and timeless elegance.

Because they are so versatile, neutrals can be used anywhere in the home. They can act as a gentle and supportive environment that allows you maximum flexibility in both your moods and your lifestyle. A neutral color scheme is therefore a good choice for shared

Living entirely with neutrals can indeed require a certain amount of self-discipline because if a room is filled with clutter this will detract from the peaceful elegance a reduced palette offers. But although neutrals lend themselves to a quieter and clutter-free environment, they do not have to be cold and formal. The best way to ensure that a neutral scheme does not become bland and lifeless is to bring in seasonal colors through accessories. For example, a simple glass vase or bowl of fruit can instantly lift a neutral room and introduce a vibrant point of focus.

HOW NEUTRALS AFFECT A ROOM

A neutral hue is not necessarily just a tone of gray or brown, but also describes any color

use neutrals to

- create a
  sense of peace
  and calm

- make a room feel
  light and airy

- increase the
  depth of a room

- highlight accent
  colors

- bring a sense
  of timeless
  elegance

- create a relaxed
  environment
  that is easy
  to live in

below Minimalist living and esthetic beauty are enhanced by the touches of black lacquer on the dividing screens that give definition and provide points of focus in this flexible space.

that recedes into the background when placed next to a contrasting color. In a whole room painted dark green with a few red accents, green becomes neutral as attention is focused on the touches of the contrasting red, rather than on the rest of the room. Like most light colors, pale neutrals reflect a good amount of natural light but, unlike clear hues, they create a much softer effect that is gentle on the eye. If neutrals that are similar in tone are placed next to one another, the colors blend together and the edges become blurred, giving objects in the room a less sharp appearance. This effect mimics the soft, natural light

found in parts of the world at high latitudes where the sun's rays have to pass through more of the atmosphere to reach the earth. Soft neutrals placed together will harmonize both the outside and inside of your home.

White is considered part of a neutral palette and creates an atmosphere that is clean and sparkling. Light neutrals are less stark while still maintaining a feeling of space and airiness, and dark neutrals can be used to enlarge the appearance of a room by increasing its depth. Contrasting dark neutrals with light tones uses areas of shadow to create a room that appears relaxed and natural.

FOR OTHER WARMING OR COZY
COLORS, SEE ALSO:

RED COCOON **54**

GOLDEN GLOW **72**

PEACHES AND CREAM **78**

GOLDEN CORN **112**

fall **hues**

We never think of fall colors as being entirely neutral. However, many of these hues fall within the brown range. Gold, orange, russet, and mahogany are all colors found in fall leaves and these deep, rich tones can be a wonderful source of inspiration that will add vibrancy to a basic neutral scheme.

When the summer ends we instinctively feel the need to retreat indoors and hibernate for the winter. Deep, rich colors remind us of warmth and sunshine, so it is not surprising that they become very attractive to us at this time of year. Yellow, pale gold, and copper

right Colorwashing on a wall adds color and texture to a neutral seating area, creating a more inviting and enclosed space that is welcome during the cooler months.

color palette

right Varying tones of cream, warm tan, and rich chocolate bring a seasonal feeling of luxury and depth into a small room.

left Light timber units and concealed lighting bring warmth to this urban kitchen while still maintaining its sleek, modern lines.

make excellent wall colors during the darker days of winter. They do not reflect as much light as paler colors, but they nevertheless make a room cheerful and welcoming. Contrasting these deep colors in the same or adjacent families on the color wheel forms a rich tapestry that will set off any decorating style. In a traditional sitting room, choose soft, luscious fabrics for drapes and upholstery or incorporate warm chenille throws and velvet cushions for an air of richness

and comfort. In a modern setting, choose tan, rust, and brown textured materials such as suede and wool.

Fiery tones are not the only colors of fall. This time of year also brings forth a variety of deep-blue- and purple-colored fruits and berries. Combining several autumnal colors such as these is a foolproof way of achieving a harmonious color scheme as the cooler tones of indigo and violet bring a more luxurious and comforting quality into the home.

FOR OTHER GROUNDING OR
EARTHY COLORS, SEE ALSO:

RUSTIC EARTH **86**

NEUTRAL SPIRIT **214**

right This beautiful
stone bathtub is
the focal point of
the bathroom and
is both pleasing to
the eye and warm
to the touch.

wood and **stone**

color palette

A neutral color scheme is not always an easy option because a lot of thought needs to go into the choice of materials. For example, one of the best ways to bring a neutral color scheme to life is to use the intriguing textures and finishes found in natural materials such as stone, plaster, canvas, and linen to provide visual and sensory stimulation. This effect can be just as appealing as a room decorated in bright colors.

Most natural materials have their own subtle colors that combine well. Wood and stone are both beautiful, natural materials that will give a feeling of permanence and strength to your home and prevent a quiet color scheme from looking pale and uninteresting. Stone and timber are often used within the building structure itself. If exposed, they will lend character to a home.

If your home has plastered walls, you can still set off neutral colors with stone flooring and wooden furniture. Stone has been used for building for centuries and is a beautiful and long-lasting natural material. It also comes in many subtle shades of sand, buff, and gray and is best used for flooring. Choose a color that blends with the architectural style and building materials in your home.

Some older properties have stone fireplaces but if you decide to use stone for a focal point you can always purchase a modern reproduction or design a modern interpretation of your own.

Wood is perhaps the most beautiful of all building materials. It combines both strength and flexibility and comes in many different colors—from the palest ash and birch to rich red mahogany. There are very few interiors that would not be enhanced with the use of wood and because of the inexhaustible number of different types of furniture available there is always something to complement your style and color scheme. A neutral background can really set off the beauty of wood and timber, which will bring depth and interest to a neutral room.

left The informal placement of contrasting colors and textures of natural materials creates a vibrant, sensuous, and creative space.

color palette

right Strong vertical
lines and striking
color contrast
create an eye-catching
central feature that
can be enjoyed from
many different angles.

sharp **contrasts**

One of the most effective ways to achieve a sense of drama in a home is to use two contrasting colors. Interiors using sharp contrasts are often favored by creative people who are searching for an esthetically beautiful home rather than a comfortable one. But it is important to bear in mind that striking contrasts can be tiring on the eye, so it is often better to reserve such a definitive color scheme for a single room or area in the home.

Black and white is a classic combination that has been featured in many different interiors through the ages. The Ancient Greeks and Romans used black-and-white tiles and wall friezes to great effect, and later, the Victorians also favored checkerboard tiles or patterns with strong contrasting borders.

Art Deco continued the trend for black and white with the addition of mirrored surfaces that accentuated the sharp contrasts. Victorian-style black-and-white bathrooms are still popular today. However, it is important when using this combination to make sure the room is large enough to take a definite pattern and to select appropriate old-style sanitary ware. Contrasting color schemes can be easier

on the eye when they include one warm and one cool color. Red and green work well together, as do yellow and blue. These combinations create a lively, vibrant atmosphere. More muted tones give a sophisticated and subdued effect.

If you want to be bold, complementary colors instill movement and energy into a room, and if the tones are varied, the effect will be well-balanced and pleasing.

FOR OTHER VIBRANT OR BOLD
COLORS, SEE ALSO:

ROYAL WELCOME **46**

THE SPIRIT OF YELLOW **92**

below Warm blue units enhance the natural beauty of the timber table, and together these colors create a relaxed and informal kitchen–diner.

sweet **pastels**

FOR OTHER EXCITING OR
ENERGETIC COLORS, SEE ALSO:

THE SPIRIT OF ORANGE **68**

EXOTIC SPICE **104**

SHOCKING PINK **204**

color palette

Pastel colors have an appealing sweet and creamy quality. Soft, light colors are often associated with children and convey a feeling of youthful enthusiasm.

During the stylish 1950s, pastels were all the rage and everything from kitchen appliances to automobiles were produced in pastel pink, lilac blue, and green. The freshness of pastels came as a light relief after the war years and reflected the more positive attitude to life. They also became a favorite of the rich and famous who made their homes in Hollywood and the Caribbean islands. We still enjoy the feel-good factor of pastels today.

Used inside and outside the home they conjure up a carefree and relaxed lifestyle.

Woodwork and timber floors painted in pastels can quickly bring a dark and old-fashioned room back to life. Their light appearance means they look good together and can be used not only on walls but on floors and ceilings too. Mix warm and cool pastels together to stop them from looking too sickly and sugary, or use a warm dove-gray or off-white for contrast.

The white within pastel colors makes paints look thicker and more opaque, but pastels are also effective for colorwashing

right The dramatic feature fireplace and hearth, mother-of-pearl bowl, and shiny surfaces work together to create a special atmosphere in this eclectic bathroom.

below Restrained
use of color featuring
pale blue-gray and
cream reflects a
simple Shaker style
that is fresh and
uncomplicated.

and broken paint effects. For example, timber floors or furniture painted with pastels will look as if it has been naturally bleached in the sun.

Although most of us think of pastels as being bright and youthful, they can also be subtle and sophisticated. For example, tones of mother-of-pearl and shimmering pearly finishes can transform a "girly" bedroom into a romantic boudoir, or turn a dark living room into a stylish and luxurious space.

all white, **all right**

The absence of color in a winter landscape gives it a dreamlike quality and so all-white rooms tend to look a little unreal. However, it is possible to exploit the theatrical appearance of a white room to make a fashion statement. Therefore, white schemes are often seen in the homes of the famous.

An all-white scheme can provide a private place in which to relax and "space out." The simplicity of white is always eye-catching and intriguing, giving a room a feeling of purity and innocence. White walls can make a room look bright and airy, but if you restrict your furniture and furnishings to shades of white, you will also create a sacred space that has to be treated with care and respect.

The secret to decorating entirely in white is to incorporate many different natural materials and textures within the room, bringing the room to life in a subtle and interesting way. To prevent starkness and glare, avoid brilliant white and instead go for off-white, pale cream, or beige, which are softer and more natural and won't look too harsh and cold at night. For most people, an all-white room is just not practical and if you

above Sometimes the simplest things can really make a difference, such as this set of plain white ceramic items.

right Strong lines and high contrasts focus the eye, define the area, and bring the large, cold space down to earth.

do not keep the room clutter-free, neat, and tidy it will soon look shoddy and dull.

So, unless you have a space that you can keep clean, or one that can become a special retreat, it is better to use white in conjunction with other colors. White creates a fresh, clean atmosphere in a room, especially if contrasted with warm, natural tones. A bed dressed in crisp, white linen seems much more inviting if the white fabrics are contrasted against a carved-wood headboard, while a living room decorated in white will look more elegant if set against a richly polished wooden floor.

above Concealed lighting and a large mirror throw an even light that enhances the subtle tones of white used in this bathroom.

inspiration

Unless you have plenty of time to experiment, it is difficult to know exactly how a room will look. Whether you are a seasoned decorator or a beginner, it is a good idea to get your creative juices flowing by looking at inspirational pictures of room settings. This chapter features illustrations of color schemes for every room so that you can see the effects of different colors and coordinating options. For those who do not have time to redecorate an entire room, this chapter also includes some quick solutions to the most common decorating problems.

living room

As this is the most used and sociable area of your home, its decor should appeal to a range of tastes and suit a variety of activities—from reading to socializing.

You are likely to spend more time in the living room than in any other area of your home, so it is important that you can live with this area for some time without the need for a change. Living rooms are usually the most spacious, well-lit, and well-furnished part of your home and so deserve careful attention when it comes to choosing a color scheme.

The living room is the main social area of a home, and one that offers you the best opportunity for self-expression—reflecting who you are. It is the perfect place to decorate in your favorite colors because when we are surrounded by colors we like, we are able to relax and feel good. However, if your living area is to be esthetically pleasing and comfortable, you also need to be sympathetic to the room itself and to harmonize these needs with your personal preferences.

You will first need to take into account the size, orientation, and style of the room and whether it has good or bad natural light.

A large room will give you more options when it comes to choosing a color scheme, while the colors in a small room need to be considered more carefully in order to accentuate its size. Patterns and large blocks of color are in scale with bigger spaces and you can break up the surfaces with paint effects or hang wallpaper to make a large room look less intimidating. A dark, cold living room would benefit from warm, light colors to make it more welcoming, while a hot, stuffy room can be made more comfortable if decorated in cooler tones.

If you have an older style or period home, you will also need to take into account both its architecture and locality. You can accentuate its features by sticking mainly to traditional colors or create a more personal and eclectic mix of new and old.

If there is only one living room in your home, it will certainly have to be a multifunctional area—a comfortable place to

opposite Moveable, colorful objects are a good way of personalizing an open-plan space and reflecting your changing moods.

right Neutral colors on the walls, combined with the browns of the flooring and furniture, create a traditional look. The red chairs provide successful accent colors.

entertain guests and family, as well as a quiet retreat in which you can relax. This dual role needs to be reflected in the decor. To achieve this, choose a contrasting color scheme that includes a mixture of warm and cool tones. The warm colors will give the room a friendly vibrancy, while the cool tones will ensure it is relaxing. Lighting will also be an important consideration, as it can quickly change the atmosphere. Having a variety of lighting options in a living room can provide both good overall light and mood lighting.

Homes with more than one living room offer you the chance to create more distinctive color schemes that will enhance your enjoyment of each space. A formal living room is more impressive and dramatic if strong, contrasting colors are used, but more calm and relaxing if decorated in cool, harmonizing colors. Large family rooms are often the center of activity in a home and bright, happy colors will instill energy and help you

right Layering color tones and introducing different textures to a neutral color palette make an easy-to-live-in space that has a timeless quality.

enjoy these rooms to the full. Rich, warm shades would make a small room or den cozier. Conservatories and pool rooms are also living areas that offer us a real chance to relax and unwind. If the colors in these areas are fresh and light, they will bring the outside in and offer a more intimate and informal entertainment area, or just a place to sit on your own.

As the living room is usually a shared space, the most difficult problem is finding colors to suit all of its users. Living with colors you find unappealing or oppressive has a negative impact on relationships, so try to avoid colors that anybody especially dislikes. A good solution is to decorate your living room in a neutral palette and add touches of accent colors. These seasonal touches are easy to change when you get tired of them and you can usually find a mix of colors to suit everyone in your home.

below Multicolored pictures make a dramatic centerpiece over this white sofa without distracting from the light and airy style.

quick solutions

- In a single living room, always combine cold and warm colors.

- Add hot colors to give vitality and life to a living room.

- Add cool colors for a quieter and more relaxing atmosphere.

- In a large living room, paint one wall a dramatic color.

- Combine small patterns and light colors in a small room.

- Neutrals with colored accents work well in shared spaces.

Though the kitchen is one of the most practical spaces in your home, it can also offer many wonderful opportunities for inspired decorating schemes. A utilitarian kitchen can be a joy to work in but the

have plenty of storage space. For example, a large kitchen can sometimes be a disadvantage because unless it is well laid out you may find yourself rushing to and fro between fridge and sink, or from the stove to the

kitchen

With careful planning and design, a kitchen becomes more than just a work area but a place of creativity and a popular venue for family and friends.

kitchen is also the heart of the home, a place where you can nurture yourself, your family, and friends. It should be a sensory place that provides plenty of tactile and creative inspiration and enjoyment. Unlike other rooms, where the wall colors are all important, there are many different elements in a kitchen that work together to create an overall effect. The colors and materials you use for the flooring, walls, counter tops, kitchen units, and appliances should blend with and enhance one another to create the right atmosphere.

A change of color can give new life to a tired kitchen, but it won't make a badly planned kitchen more comfortable to work in. Before you start decorating make sure that you are happy with the layout and that you

preparation area. On the other hand, a small, cramped kitchen can feel claustrophobic and it is therefore often a good idea to open it up into another room by installing a half wall or breakfast bar. Decide whether you want to keep the existing units or not. If the layout works for you, you may be able to retain the units but replace the door fronts, or just paint them a different color.

The style and orientation of your home is important when deciding on a color scheme. A large kitchen can look cold and uninviting without some bright, warm colors, as these will give it a more social atmosphere and encourage the family to congregate there. Mid or darker tones or patterns are best for flooring as they show the dirt less, but if you

opposite The pale lilac walls enhance these beautiful wood-grained units without overpowering the room to create a timeless style.

above The large
painting creates a focal
point as you enter this
galley kitchen and helps
create the illusion
of a wider space.

want to keep the floor light, go for a light timber, or checkered or marbled-effect tile. A multicolored environment looks wonderful in a farmhouse kitchen and is especially supportive if you like cooking. Rich-colored wall tiles can add sparkle and a sense of fun

to a family kitchen, as can brightly colored storage jars, utensils, and blinds.

In a small kitchen, which can become stuffy and hot, keep colors light and cool. Avoid using brilliant white for walls and units, as this causes glare that makes a room tiring and uncomfortable to be in for any length of time. Off-white and pastel colors are a better choice for countertops, walls, or tiles, as these make the room look larger and more airy. If you already have white units, stick to light-colored timber for flooring and counters or contrast the white with colored tiles and walls. Good lighting is also very important in a small area, so, if possible, include counter-top lighting under the wall units.

For the serious or professional cook, a more streamlined kitchen with muted colors may be less distracting. Here, the materials used within the kitchen can create interesting contrasts in color. For example, a combination of stainless steel, timber, marble, or granite

work surfaces can provide an efficient but stimulating environment. Units are best kept simple in design, and in one color, so that they are easier to keep clean. If you decide on a monochrome scheme, you can make it more interesting by adding contrasting colors in kitchen equipment and accessories.

below Unusual displays of fruit and vegetables are a quick and easy way to bring color and life to a sleek, modern kitchen.

quick solutions

- Repaint tired cupboard doors in a cream, blue, or light-green eggshell or gloss paint.

- Give kitchen walls a new lease on life by using a colorwash or paint effect over the old color.

- A new white counter will instantly reflect more light into a dark kitchen.

- Over-tiling old wall tiles in rich, deep colors will add more vitality and interest.

- Colorful accessories such as blinds, utensils, and jars in contrasting tones can give character to a functional space.

- A laminate timber floor can quickly be installed over an old floor to make a kitchen more spacious and modern.

Often the most undervalued room in the house, the bathroom can really come into its own with an injection of well-chosen colors. Bathrooms are often thought of as rooms serving a single purpose but they

Bathing has long been associated with the therapeutic qualities of water, cleansing the body, and reducing mental and emotional stress. The benefits of water are not just a myth, as water is closely linked with the

bathroom

Whether purely functional or a place to luxuriate, your bathroom should be a well-planned and attractively decorated room.

opposite Cream and gray make an unusual and restrained combination for a bathroom that is simple but sophisticated. The timber floor helps lead the eye to adjoining rooms to create a more spacious feel.

can have several different functions. For example, a private bathroom or *en suite* is a quiet retreat where you can unwind, while a family bathroom is a busy utilitarian space. And bathing is not only about relaxation, as an invigorating shower can leave you feeling fresh and full of vitality.

moon and its effects on seasonal cycles and tidal rhythms. Our body is made up of between 60 and 70 percent water, and so our internal rhythms and moods are strongly affected by the moon. As a result, we are very sensitive to the movement of water. The colors in your bathroom can really support these mood-enhancing qualities. Even the blue color of water is itself therapeutic.

Decorating your bathroom in colors reminiscent of water can really improve the way you use and enjoy your bathroom. Cool colors make a bathroom look fresh and clean. Aquamarine, dark blue, and sea green are particularly suitable. As reminders of revitalizing places by the sea, rivers, or lakes, they can help create a positive frame of mind. In

right The strong, simple shapes and shiny surfaces of the faucets and wash basins enhance a subtle color scheme.

color therapy, blue is associated with the throat and lungs, and our ability to express ourselves verbally. This releasing effect of water is demonstrated when we instinctively sing or whistle in the shower.

White is another color associated with water, and particularly with its cleansing power. Though an all-white bathroom can feel cold and utilitarian, when blue and white are combined, this conjures up images of the breaking surf and so gives a bathroom extra vitality and sparkle. Black and white has long been a popular choice for bathrooms, and can

look particularly stylish in more formal locations. Period bathrooms can also look good in black and white. However, this tends to suggest Victorian attitudes to bathing and so we are less likely to linger in a period bathroom decorated in this color. To make such a bathroom more appealing, include thick, fluffy towels and robes in warm colors.

Bathing while surrounded by nature is an enjoyable experience for most of us. Natural materials such as wood, and moisture-loving plants in your bathroom help to create an exotic and relaxing space, and this warm nurturing effect can be further enhanced with the introduction of soothing colors such as terracotta, peach, or dusky pink.

Colors in the ocher, tan, and brown ranges are in natural harmony with most skin tones, and when you look in the mirror they will give you a more healthy appearance. Lighting also affects the way you look, and bad lighting can even undermine your self-esteem. For example, fluorescent lights have a blue tinge that can make you appear tired and ill. So chose light bulbs that have a yellow or peachy tint. Clean, white, low-voltage halogen lights are highly effective when located over a mirror but they are also very bright and so you will need to include some soft mood-lighting near the tub.

If space permits, create a relaxation area in your bathroom, or indeed elsewhere in your home. This area could include a home gym, sauna, hot tub, or Jacuzzi. By including a relaxed seating area, you can create a social center in much the same way as did the ancient Egyptians and Romans. Keep a selection of bottles of colored, aromatic bath salts and oils, as well as some plants with good foliage, on a shelf or table.

quick solutions

- Blue and white are classic bathroom colors that look clean and fresh.

- Add a border of colored tiles or mosaics to an all-white bathroom.

- Make a bathroom more friendly with green plants, soaps, and decorative bottles.

- Add warm-colored towels and fluffy bath mats to a cold bathroom.

- Moisture-loving plants can create a more exotic and relaxing space.

- Soft lighting and warm colors will make you look healthier in the mirror.

below Shimmering steel and glass create a moving play of light in a small shower room that would otherwise be dull and uninteresting.

Your bedroom is the first place you see when you wake up in the morning and the last at night, so the colors around you will have a powerful effect on your body and mind. This private space gives you the opportunity to choose colors that have special, personal appeal. But first you need to decide whether you want your bedroom to be a quiet haven or a place to pamper yourself and tantalize your senses.

Cool colors create a calm and soothing atmosphere that is especially welcome if you find it difficult to get a good night's sleep. Light tones of blue and green are relaxing to the mind and have been found to slow down our body systems, and so can help fight stress. Darker shades of blue mimic the night sky and have a more sedative effect. These colors unlock the unconscious mind and promote vivid dreams, and when teamed with purple, silver, and gold, will create an air of mystery and imagination.

Though the bedroom is primarily a place to rest and sleep, it is also the first choice of room for making love. So while the colors in the bedroom should be soothing and relaxing, they also need to energize and inspire you. Soft, warm colors like pink, peach, tan, and cream are emotionally relaxing and have a gentle, soothing quality that will make you feel comfortable and safe, and so less guarded and more sensitive to your own feelings as well as those of your partner. Deep pink, red, and violet are all colors associated with love, and a bedroom decorated in these tones will become a sensual boudoir where you can enjoy being pampered and celebrate your sexuality.

If, like most people, you want to create a bedroom that is both relaxing and energizing, it is a good idea to choose a soft light or neutral tone for the main wall color and add touches of deep, rich tones on the bed and furnishings. If you have a variety of bed

bedroom

The modern bedroom is a multifunctional room associated with both peace and passion where you can refresh body and mind and indulge your fantasies.

opposite A touch of pattern and color in the Roman blinds and black iron bedstead is all that is needed to lift this cool and tranquil bedroom.

covers and linens, you can dress your bed in different colors depending on your mood.

White is a popular choice for bedrooms, as it gives a room a sense of peace, purity, and calmness. Crisp white bed linen is always a joy to sleep in, as it feels fresh and cool, and because white is a neutral color, it balances the psyche and has good regenerative powers. On its own, white can be cold and clinical, but combined with fresh country prints or natural wood furniture and flooring it can make a cool, dreamy bedroom.

We need to feel safe and secure when we sleep and this is why we prefer to sleep in upstairs rooms with a good view of the door from our bed. If you have a downstairs bedroom, decorating in pale sky colors creates the illusion of being high up, while deeper colors can help give a sense of protected space in a large, open bedroom. A four-poster bed is another way of creating a protected space within your bedroom. Drape the bed with natural muslin or colorful silks for a more exotic feel.

opposite The light-reflecting materials and colors of floors and ceilings play an important role in creating the tranquil and airy atmosphere in this bedroom.

left Varying the tones of a related color family creates a comfortable and harmonious room.

A FEW SUITABLE DINING ROOM
COLORS INCLUDE:

ROYAL WELCOME **46**

GOLDEN GLOW **72**

RUSTIC EARTH **86**

EMERALD RICH **172**

Whether formal or relaxed, the dining room provides an opportunity to go for a dynamic and interesting color scheme. Eating should be an enjoyable and sociable activity. The colors around you will mood can easily be changed by using different-colored table decorations. A classic white cloth always looks good and you can ring the changes with colorful table runners, glassware, or crockery.

dining room

Whether formal or informal, eating areas are the most important social centers in your home, where you can enjoy a meal and relax with family and friends.

opposite Introducing multicolored chairs is a fun, informal way of defining the central area of this large dining room.

have a marked influence on whether you eat to live or live to eat.

As our attitudes to meal times have changed, most of us now have several different eating areas in the home. A formal dining area is a place that is probably used only for entertaining or for special occasions, so a dramatic scheme here will look both elegant and gracious. A large, formal dining room can look awesome with striped or patterned wallpaper, polished furniture, and large mirrors. Dark colors reflect little natural light, but if the room is used mostly in the evenings, a wall color such as deep green can give a feeling of enclosure and protection. If

right Dark green is used on the wall to create a protected space in this eating nook.

you prefer warm colors, a deep red, ocher, or burnt orange will glow in candlelight. The

Many families eat in the kitchen or have a breakfast bar if the room is open plan. Warm colors are more relaxed and therefore particularly suitable for informal kitchen dining, and a hard-wearing table and chairs are essential. Wooden tables have a friendly glow that is welcome in a farmhouse-style or family kitchen but can look good in a

contemporary setting too. Entertaining in the kitchen can be relaxed and enjoyable but your guests do not necessarily want to see piles of dishes. Low lighting over a kitchen table can therefore make dining in the kitchen more intimate, and you can make a kitchen table more attractive by including colorful tablemats and informal bunches of flowers or herbs.

Dining rooms that are open plan with the living room are often under-used, as many people feel uncomfortable eating at a table in the middle of a room. Warm colors are more conducive to eating, as they remind us of the safety and comfort of eating around a fire. Create a more protected space using a contrasting floor rug and low-level lighting to make the room feel more cozy.

If an archway or wide doorway links the living room and dining areas, you need to keep continuity of color between the rooms. Painting the walls of the dining area a deeper

below The orange tones in this room reflect a warm glow at night and also set off the rich timber dining furniture during the day.

tone than the walls in your living room ensures that the rooms remain linked, but with the dining area appearing more inviting.

Nooks can also be transformed into cozy and comfortable eating areas. If a nook is separate from the kitchen and living room, it is possible to make it a cool, natural space by decorating it in more muted tones for a fresh and airy feel. Provided that there is natural light, plants are a good addition as the foliage will make the space look soft and relaxing.

quick solutions

- A colorful table runner and seat pads can lift a dull dining room instantly.

- Leafy plants will create a more relaxed and natural eating area.

- A pendant light over a dining table evokes a more intimate atmosphere.

- Turn off kitchen lights and use candles when you are dining at a kitchen table.

- Keep breakfast nooks light and airy by using soft pastels or warm neutrals.

- Create timeless elegance in a formal dining room with deep, rich contrasting tones.

- Warm colors are more sociable and make a dining area feel cozier.

above Reflections on the glass table mirror the outside view and bring pattern and movement to this formal dining room.

A FEW SUITABLE STUDY OR HOME
OFFICE COLORS INCLUDE:

RED COCOON **54**

FALL HUES **218**

WOOD AND STONE **220**

SWEET PASTELS **224**

Having a dedicated work area in the home is a growing trend. Choosing the right color schemes will very much depend on the type of work you do as well as the size and location of your home office.

shutters are useful to cut down bright sunlight during the day, or you could introduce a more colorful sun-filtering blind.

A study can become a cozy haven if filled with comfy chairs, interesting books, pictures,

study or home office

It may be a mainly functional place, but the study or office also needs to be a well-planned and inspiring room that reflects the type of work you do.

right You do not need to set aside an entire room as a home office. It can be housed in any convenient area, for example, within a living room or bedroom. It should incorporate plenty of storage, be light, and well lit.

Studies are most often located in a spare bedroom, but you may also accommodate a work area in a loft, mezzanine, or outbuilding.

If your study is a separate room, you have many different decorating options. If you use your study mainly for office- and computer-based work, it will need to be well lit and more functional than a study used for reading or creative pursuits. Cool, clear colors or pastels are less distracting when you need to concentrate and these hues also look good when combined with contemporary-style furniture and fittings. If you opt for a more homely feel to your study, warm neutrals combine well with wooden furniture and you can add either natural or painted shelving and bookcases. Slatted timber blinds or

and other inspirational objects. Painting this kind of space in bright, rich tones will make you feel comfortable and cocooned. Rich, warm tones are also suitable for a formal library, especially if the room has a feature fireplace or wood paneling. Good overhead lighting as well as old-fashioned brass reading lamps will complete the classic look.

When it comes to decorating, workrooms are often sadly neglected. Consequently, these important areas quickly become filled with clutter and are little used. You will be encouraged to spend more time there if you make workshops and studios bright and attractive spaces. Choose your favorite colors to make these areas vibrant and full of vitality.

above The blue sleeper couch and paper lamp make a home office more comfortable and less impersonal so that it can also be used as a guest bedroom.

index

Numbers in italics refer to illustrations.

picture credits & acknowledgments

Dominic Blackmore/Ideal Home/IPC Syndication: front jacket, 57.
Elizabeth Whiting & Associates: back jacket, 20–1, 30–3, 43, 45–6, 55, 60–3, 69, 70, 72, 74, 80–1, 95–6, 99, 101, 104, 110–11, 113, 115, 121–2, 125, 127–35, 138–41, 146, 164, 166–7, 169–71, 178, 185, 187–8, 195–7, 200–8, 210–11, 218–20, 223–5, 235, 237–9, 241–2, 245, 249, 250, 253.
zapaimages: 79, 106–8, 124–5, 156, 215, 232–3, 247, 251–2.

The author would like to thank everyone at Axis Publishing involved in producing this book. Thank you to all the color practitioners and Color Associations working to bring a new awareness of the effects and benefits of color in our lives and especially in our homes.